Interior Sketches I

Ramblings around Interior Alaska historic sites

Text and drawings by Ray Bonnell

Pingo Press - Fairbanks, Alaska

Artwork, graphics and text copyright 2023 by Ray Bonnell.

All rights reserved. No part of this publication may be reproduced, stored in a retrieved system, or transmitted in any form or by any means—electronic, mechanical, photocopying, or otherwise—without the prior written permission of the publisher.

All drawings and essays related to specific historic sites were originally published in *Sketches of Alaska,* a biweekly column appearing in the *Fairbanks Daily News-Miner.* Some of the essays have been revised and expanded since original publication.

Book design, layout and formatting done at Pingo Press. Fonts used: Licinia Aged, Gil Sans, Minion Pro

Cover illustration: Black Rapids Roadhouse (see page 16)

Frontispiece: Northern Commerical Company warehouses, Fairbanks (see page 104)

This book would not have been possible without the support of my wife, Betsy, who has been my companion for fifty years, and voluntarily (yes—voluntarily) edits my work and acts as an artistic consultant; and the willingness of my first editor at the *Fairbanks Daily News-Miner,* Glenn BurnSilver, to give me a chance to show what I could do.

127 Glacier Avenue. Fairbanks, AK 99701
info@pingopress.us

Printed in the United States of America
Second Edition, Revised and Updated, April 2023
ISBN 978-1-7364236-3-9

Contents

Map 1

Introduction 2

Fort Egbert brought order to Alaska-Canada border 4
        Eagle, Taylor Highway

Eagle courthouse dates back to early days of Territorial justice 6
        Eagle, Taylor Highway

Exploring Boundary and the Top of the World Highway 8
        Boundary, Top of the World Highway

Episcopal Church establishes St. Timothy's and Tanacross 100 years ago 10
        Tanacross, Alaska Highway

Dot Lake community grew from Alaska Highway construction camp 12
        Dot Lake, Alaska Highway

Alcan construction equipment cached in Delta Junction 14
        Delta Junction, Alaska Highway

Historic roadhouse at Black Rapids escapes destruction 16
        Black Rapids, Richardson Highway

Big Delta WAMCATS station helped link Fairbanks to the world 18
        Big Delta, Richardson Highway

John Haines homestead still provides inspiration 20
        Richardson, Richardson Highway

Little remains of Richardson Roadhouse and community around it 22
        Richardson, Richardson Highway

Salcha Native Cemetery, a people and place worth remembering 24
        Salcha, Richardson Highway

Log cabin post office one of few buildings left along Valdez Creek 26
        Valdez Creek, Denali Highway

Denali National Park dog feed cache reflects park's mushing history 28
        Headquarters, Denali National Park & Preserve

Kantishna's Busia cabin exudes Alaskan ambiance 30
        Kantishna, Denali National Park & Preserve

Contents

Historic Healy Hotel lives on at new location..32
   Healy, Parks Highway

St. Mark's Episcopal Church a reminder of Nenana's early history..34
   Nenana, Parks Highway

Taku Chief a relic of Civil Aeronautics Administration's riverboat days......................................36
   Nenana, Parks Highway

Ester assay office, a little building that endured..38
   Ester, Parks Highway

At the Malemute Saloon...40
   Ester, Parks Highway

Manley's Northern Commercial Company store filled with memories.......................................42
   Manley, Elliott Highway

Mining camps merge to form Livengood in 1915..44
   Livengood, Elliott Highway

Olnes Outhouse has distinctive character..46
   Olnes, Elliott Highway

Gold Dredge No. 8, a giant that helped save Fairbanks..48
   Fox, Steese Highway

Fairbanks Creek: mining camps, churn drills and gold dredges..50
   Fairbanks Creek, Steese highway

Meandering mining camp? Where is Meehan?..52
   Fairbanks Creek, Steese Highway

All that's left of Eldorado...54
   Little Eldorado Creek, Steese Highway

Leonhard Seppala's Chatanika cabin, a link to one of dog mushing's greats...............................56
   Chatanika, Steese Highway

Chatanika schoolhouse, a historic preservation success story..58
   Chatanika, Steese Highway

Ambitious Davidson Ditch brought water to Fairbanks dredges..60
   U.S. Creek, Steese highway

Museum at Central, Alaska displays early dog sled development...62
   Central, Steese highway

Contents

A haunting end to life at Circle Hot Springs **64**
    Circle Hot Springs, Steese Highway

Find memories, welcome and soothing waters at Chena Hot Springs **66**
    Chena Hot Springs, Chena Hot Springs Road

Old City Hall part of downtown Fairbanks modernization **68**
    Downtown Fairbanks, Cushman Street

The Fairbanks Lacey Street Theater, grand building on a budget **70**
    Downtown Fairbanks, 2nd Avenue

Pioneer Hotel no longer stands, but history remains **72**
    Downtown Fairbanks, 1st Avenue

Fairbanks' historic Masonic Temple is no more **74**
    Downtown Fairbanks, 1st Avenue

First Avenue bathhouse a home for many different groups **76**
    Downtown Fairbanks, 1st Avenue

The Falcon Joslin House, vestige of a builder's dream **78**
    Downtown Fairbanks, Cowles Street

Thomas Memorial Library a civilizing influence in early Fairbanks **80**
    Downtown Fairbanks, 1st Avenue

St. Matthew's Episcopal Church retains its rustic charm **82**
    Downtown Fairbanks, 1st Avenue

Valdez-Fairbanks Trail, a lifeline for early Interior Alaskans **84**
    Pioneer Park, Pioneer Museum

Charles Adams and the SS Lavelle Young, icons of Alaska steamboating **86**
    Pioneer Park, Gold Rush Town

Palace Hotel a rare survivor of Fairbanks early business district **88**
    Pioneer Park, Gold Rush Town

Pioneer Park house offers glimpse of mysterious Kitty Hensley **90**
    Pioneer Park, Gold Rush Town

Gold Rush Town church originally graced downtown Fairbanks **92**
    Pioneer Park, Gold Rush Town

Judge Wickersham brought stability (and culture) to Fairbanks **94**
    Pioneer Park, Gold Rush Town

Contents

SS Nenana, the last steamboat to Fairbanks 96
    Pioneer Park, main entrance

The Tanana Valley Railroad and Engine No. 1, the Gold Dust Line 98
    Pioneer Park, Railroad Museum

The Alaska Road Commission, 55 years helping develop Alaska 100
    Southwest Fairbanks, Peger Road

Ben Eielson and his Jenny fly into Alaska history 102
    West Fairbanks, International Airport

Warehouse all that's left of Fairbanks Northern Commercial Company 104
    Fairbanks, Garden Island, N. Turner Street

Immaculate Conception Church a moving experience 106
    Fairbanks, Garden Island, N. Cushman Street

West Coast Grocery warehouse and a ghost of Christmas past 108
    Fairbanks, Garden Island, Driveway Street

Fairbanks coal bunkers were the last of their kind in Alaska 110
    Fairbanks, Garden Island, Phillips Field Road

Fairbanks Exploration Company revived early Fairbanks 112
    Fairbanks, Illinois Street

Remainder of Fairbanks Exploration Company housing lines Illinois Street 114
    Fairbanks, Illinois Street

Fordson snow tractor and the Detroit-Arctic Expedition 116
    Fairbanks, College Road, Fountainhead Antique Auto Museum

Creamer's Dairy an integral part of Fairbanks history and landscape 118
    Fairbanks, College Road, Creamers Field

Desjardins-Stroecker Farm representative of early Fairbanks agriculture 120
    Fairbanks, Farmers Loop, Fairbanks

Quirky Eielson building at UAF is an Art Deco gem 122
    University of Alaska, Salcha Street

UAF's Rainey-Skarland cabin rich with history 124
    University of Alaska, Kuskokwim Way

Appendix - Identification key for animal tracks found at the bottom of some pages 126

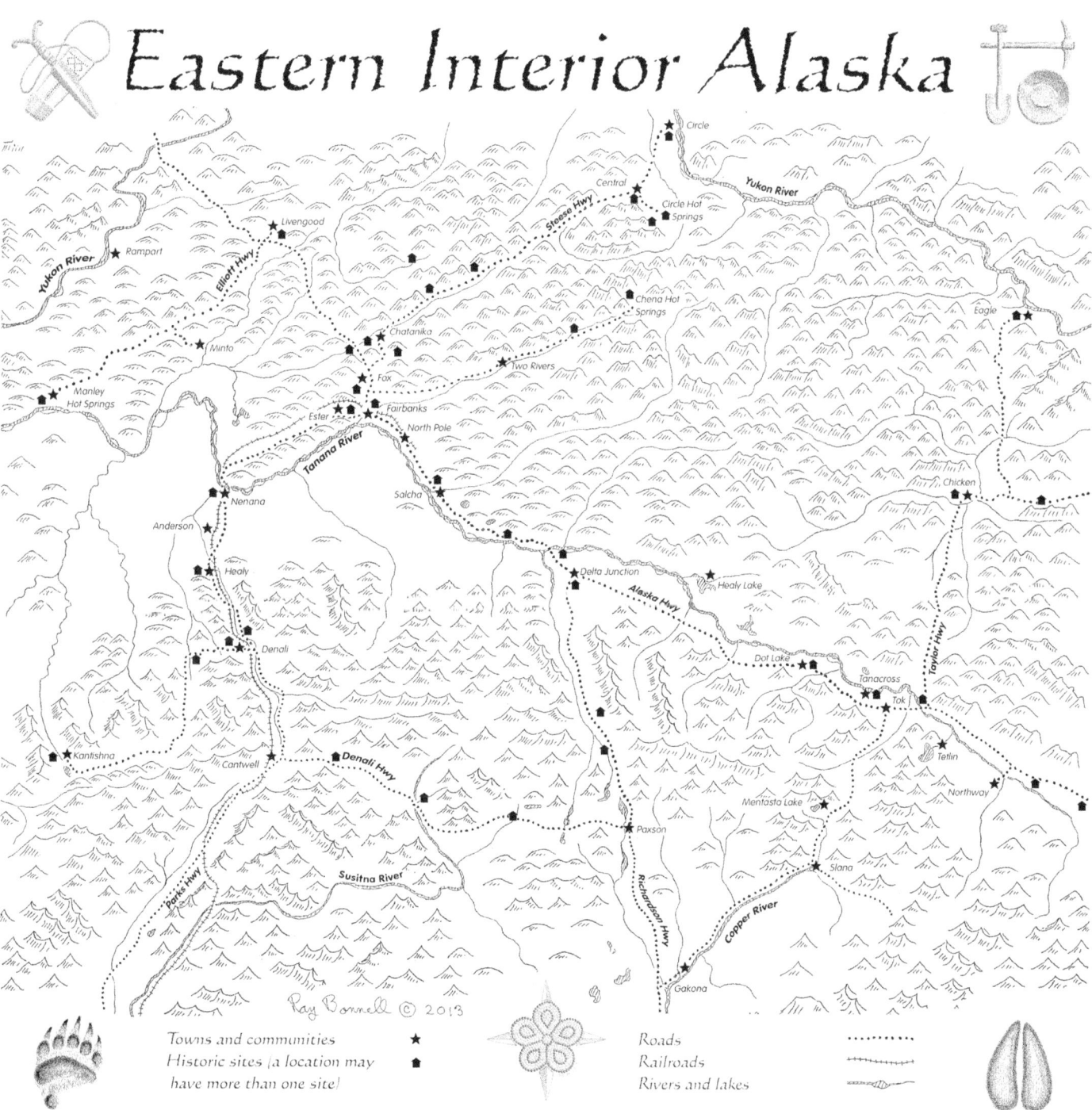

Introduction

Tanana River and Alaska Range from the ridge above John Haines homestead

Introduction

"They say that those who have lived more than a year within the interior of Alaska suffer a nostalgia that knows no cure save the return to the land they love; they feel the pull of a magnet that draws them from the busy haunts of men back to the lonesome outposts of the North."
(Thomas Rickard in *Through the Yukon and Alaska*, 1909)

My sketches of Alaska are from the section of the Eastern Interior connected to the road system. The great bow of the Yukon River as it sweeps northwest from the Canadian border and then southwest to its confluence with the Tanana River delineates its eastern, northern and westernmost points. The Alaska Range, the northernmost portions of the Susitna and Copper River Valleys, and the Wrangell Mountains form its southerly borders. Just north of the Alaska Range and snaking almost completely across the region from east to west is the 582-mile-long Tanana River. All told the region covers about 100,000 square miles, larger than many of the contiguous Unites States.

The Eastern Interior is a land of extremes. It's cold continental climate means winters are long and harsh with temperatures that can plummet to minus 60 degrees Fahrenheit and colder. Summers are all-too-short, but temperatures can climb above 90 degrees.

Introduction

Permafrost (ground that remains frozen for more than two consecutive years) defines the land. Most of the region is underlain by discontinuous permafrost, which means that only a few areas—such as some south-facing slopes and lands adjacent to rivers—are permafrost free.

Annual precipitation is rather meager— limited to about 11 inches annually. (Most snow in the Interior is dry powder snow.) Interior Alaska's annual precipitation is actually low enough to classify the area as semi-arid. What gives the region it abundant liquid water in summer is permafrost that traps water in the active soil layer above it, and a low evaporation rate.

The region is starkly beautiful; dominated by rivers, mountains, and the boreal forest. Salmon, grayling and whitefish course through its rivers and streams; and caribou, moose, black and brown bear, wolf, and myriad smaller creatures roam the land.

Save for a few pockets of humanity it is a wild, and, at least to Western sensibilities, seemingly empty land. During the time period when non-natives came into contact with the area's indigenous groups, two conflicting views of the wildlands entangled each other.

To the native Athabascan Indians the land was full. They had already attained equilibrium between their population and the land's carrying capacity. Also, for them nature abounded with the spirits of creatures they depended on— spirits the Athabascans respected and sought balance with.

Most Westerners saw the land as simply a resource-rich wilderness. In their eyes, it was empty and under-utilized. Its resources, whether game or fur-bearing animals, fish, timber, or minerals, were just commodities available for exploitation.

According to ethnographers, when Westerners first entered the region in the late 1800s there were probably no more than 1500 Athabascan Indians living here. By the first decade of the 1900s, U.S. Census figures show about 11,000 people (predominantly Westerners) calling the area home. Now, 100 years later, just over 125,000 people reside here.

Although sparsely populated, Eastern Interior Alaska is rich in history—from the Indians who have lived here for thousands of years, to the fur traders, miners, missionaries, homesteaders and other Westerners who began settling here in the 1800s.

Scattered across this region are scores of historic and culturally important sites. Although some of these sites are being preserved, many are fading away—the result of development, vandalism, accidents and time. And just as the sites are fading away, so too is their memory, as the old-timers who lived this history die or move away.

I feel it is important to at least record a "snapshot in time" of these sites. Consequently, for the past 30 years I have been tramping the roads and trails of Eastern Interior Alaska; visiting old mining camps, roadhouses, cemeteries, homesteads and villages; taking photographs and notes and producing sketches.

The sketches have become detailed pen and ink drawings, and recently, the notes have become essays. For over three years I have been producing a column entitled "Sketches of Alaska" for my local newspaper, the *Fairbanks Daily News-Miner*. Each column features one of my drawings plus a short essay describing the site.

Presented here are drawings and essays taken from the first two and a half years of my column. Many of the essays have been revised and expanded since initial publication. I have tried to make each column as historically accurate as possible, gleaning information from numerous sources including interviews with local residents and land owners. Sources for each essay are listed if you want to find out more about a site.

Being an under-employed artist operating on a shoestring budget, my travels of necessity have been restricted to sites on or very near the road system. This means that you can drive to most of these sites and see these pieces of our history. Whether you drive, walk, or sit in an easy chair, hopefully this book will serve as a guide while you do your own ramblings around Interior Alaska.

Taylor Highway, Eagle

Fort Egbert NCO Quarters in 1998

Fort Egbert brought order to Alaska-Canada border

The non-commissioned officers (NCO) quarters at Fort Egbert, Alaska is one of the few buildings remaining at the former Army post (now managed cooperatively by the U.S. Bureau of Land Management and the Eagle Historical Society and Museums).

Fort Egbert (adjacent to Eagle, Alaska) was established in response to the 1897 Klondike Gold Rush in Canada. This was a rough and tumble period. Rumors of disorder, food shortages, and lawlessness, especially on the U.S. side of the border, caused consternation when they eventually reached Washington, D.C.

The U.S. War Department investigated in 1897 and decided to establish a series of forts along the major transportation routes in Alaska and near mining regions. A fort at Eagle, Alaska (12 miles from the Canadian border) was the closest to the Klondike.

In July 1899 a contingent of about 100 Army personnel arrived in Eagle by steamer. According to BLM literature, the troops were sent to "provide law and order, protect commerce, care for impoverished miners, build roads and trails, and develop better communication with the nation." The soldiers hastily began constructing barracks, barns and other facilities before winter set in.

The next year Fort Egbert became headquarters for construction of the first telegraph line in Alaska. The Washington-Alaska Military Cable and Telegraph System (WAMCATS), built between 1900 and 1904, linked military posts in Alaska with the rest of the nation.

Maintaining the telegraph lines proved more difficult than anticipated. A 1903 U.S. War Department report lamented that although the telegraph lines were meant simply to link Alaska's military posts, almost the entire garrison of several forts (including Fort Egbert) were constantly maintaining the lines and unavailable for other duties.

More dependable and easily maintained wireless telegraph systems (radio) gradually replaced the land lines. By 1911 infantry troops were no longer needed to maintain the lines, and the Army withdrew most of its soldiers from Fort Egbert. A wireless telegraph station was operated by the Army Signal Corps there until 1925 when the station burned down.

After the Army departed, the Alaska Road Commission (ARC) took over a portion of the site. Some of the buildings were moved or salvaged—others simply fell apart. But by 1940 only five of the fort's original 45 buildings remained in decent condition. The remaining buildings included the quartermaster's storehouse, mule barn, granary, water wagon shed, and NCO quarters.

Eagle's residents have worked diligently to preserve what is left of Fort Egbert. In the 1970s they secured funding from The National Trust for Historic Preservation and the federal government. The funds were administered by BLM, and the fort's buildings were restored between 1975 and 1980. In 1975 the Eagle Historic District (including Fort Egbert) was declared a National Historic Landmark.

In 1991 the Eagle Historical Society and Museums, the City of Eagle, and the BLM signed a Cooperative Agreement to continue protecting significant cultural resources and historic properties within the Eagle Historic District National Historic Landmark.

One of the most recent projects at Fort Egbert was additional restoration work (completed in 2008) on the NCO quarters. The project included repairing original materials such as doors and floor, replicating and replacing the wallpaper, and stabilizing the building's foundation.

There were originally three NCO quarters buildings. Only one remains at the fort, but another was moved to the riverbank in 1915 (after Fort Egbert closed) and used as the Customs Service office and residence. It has also been restored as a period residence and Customs Service museum, and is open to the public.

Sources:

- *Eagle – Fort Egbert, a Remnant of the Past*. U.S. Bureau of Land Management. 2008
- "Eagle Historic District, National Register of Historic Places Registration Form." Paulette Kilmer & William Hanable. National Park Service, 1988
- 'Eagle History." Eagle Historical Society and Museums website. 2011
- *North of 53°, the Wild Days of the Alaska-Yukon Mining Frontier, 1870-1914*. William R. Hunt. MacMillan Publishing Company. 1974
- *Reports of Department and Division Commanders, for the Fiscal year ending June 30, 1903*. U.S. War Department. 1903
- *The Last Frontier: A History of the Yukon Basin of Canada and Alaska*. Melody Webb. University of New Mexico. 1985

Taylor Highway, Eagle

U.S. Courthouse in Eagle in 1998

Eagle courthouse dates back to early days of Territorial justice

On June 6, 1900, Congress enacted a civil code for the Territory of Alaska that, among other things, split Alaska's single judicial district into three districts. Eagle City (less than two years old) became the headquarters for the Third Judicial District, and James Wickersham was appointed as its sole judge.

Wickersham, his family and staff arrived in Eagle via riverboat from Dawson City on July 16, 1900. In his

1938 book, *Old Yukon: Tails, Trails and Trials*, Wickersham wrote that the entire town (about 500 people) turned out to greet them. He went on to add that in addition to Fort Egbert, (which had been established the preceding year adjacent to the town) and the numerous cabins housing the town's residents, the community consisted of several stores, a customs house, Presbyterian church, Catholic church, two restaurants, and four or five log-cabin saloons.

Wickersham and his clerk quickly set to work collecting license fees from businesses in Eagle, Circle and Rampart to fund the construction of a courthouse and jail, and by 1901 the two structures had been completed. That same year, Eagle City became the first incorporated city in Interior Alaska (and the second in the territory).

The courthouse (shown in the drawing) is a two-story wood-frame structure with shiplap siding and a gable roof. It originally had offices for the judge and his staff on the first floor, and a courtroom on the second floor. The jail, with an office for a U.S. marshal, was a separate log structure directly south of the courthouse.

Wickersham relates in his book that during winter when the Yukon River was frozen and there was negligible risk of prisoners fleeing, they were allowed to roam about town during the day, having only to return to their cells each evening. With the threat of being locked out of their warm cells at night, few if any prisoners failed to check in.

The Third Judicial District's headquarters moved to Fairbanks in 1903, but the courthouse in Eagle was maintained as a court until the 1950s. After the jail burned down (for the second time) in 1911, a room in the courthouse was used to hold prisoners, and an adjacent room was reserved for a guard.

One consequence of relocating the Third Judicial District was the marshal also moving to Fairbanks. After that the Eagle resident who apprehended a suspected criminal had to guard the prisoner until a marshal could arrive. An unintended effect was that during winter, when the trip to Eagle was long and arduous, few arrests were made.

During the 1950s the city of Eagle assumed ownership of the courthouse building. From then until the 1970s the rooms allotted for the jail were kept for that function, and a portion of the first floor was used as the community library, but the rest of the ground floor was used for storage. The second-floor courtroom was preserved.

The appearance of the courthouse has changed little through the years. The covered porch on the east end of the building was torn down in 1926 due to decay, and a boardwalk along the north side of the building was removed in the 1950s for the same reason.

When the building was restored in the 1970s, the boardwalk and covered porch were rebuilt. The entire building is now operated as a museum by the city, with the courtroom on the second floor maintained in the same state as it was during Judge Wickersham's tenure.

Sources:

- "Eagle Courthouse, Architectural Data Form," Historic American Building Survey, 1986
- "Eagle Historic District, National Register of Historic Places - Registration Form." Paulette Kilmer & William Hanable. National Park Service, 1988
- *Fort Egbert and the Eagle Historic District: Results of Archaeological and Historic Research - Summer 1977.* Ann Shinkwin, Elizabeth Andrews, Russ Sackett & Mary Kroul. University of Alaska, Fairbanks. 1978
- *Fort Egbert and Eagle, a Preservation Plan.* National Trust for Historic Preservation. 1977
- *Old Yukon: Tales, Trails and Trials.* James Wickersham. Washington Law Book Company. 1938
- *Report on excavations at U.S. courthouse, Eagle, Alaska.* Ann Shinkwin & Russ Sackett. University of Alaska, Fairbanks. 1976
- *The Last Frontier: A History of the Yukon Basin of Canada and Alaska.* Melody Webb. University of New Mexico. 1985

Top-of-the-world Highway, Boundary

Boundary Roadhouse in 1998

Exploring Boundary and the Top of the World Highway

When the military road from Fort Liscum in Valdez to Fort Egbert in Eagle was "completed" in 1900 it was little more than a rough trail suitable only for saddle and pack horses. The U.S. government, primarily through the Alaska Road Commission (ARC), would struggle for the next decade to construct a bona fide road across the rough mountains south of Eagle into the Fortymile River area. Constantly short on funds, the ARC (which received a mixture of Territorial funding and direct appropriations from Congress) only made limited progress, but by 1910 it had established a rudimentary road as far south as Wade Creek, also called Jack Wade Creek.

At what is now called Jack Wade Junction, 46 miles south of Eagle, a trail took off to the east towards the Walker Fork and Canyon Creek drainages. Located about 10 miles southeast of the junction, the small hamlet of Boundary (so named because it was only three miles from the Canadian border) served miners in the Walker Fork drainage. The community was also called Walker Fork and there may have been a Boundary "North" (on the ridge above the creek, where the roadhouse is) and "South" (one mile south on the bank of Walker Fork, where several dredges operated).

There appears to be scant information about the camp except that it had a roadhouse, and its post office was established in 1940 (lasting until 1956). The U.S. Bureau of Land Management publication, *Taylor Highway, Fortymile Gold Country*, states that Boundary was established sometime in the 1890s and the roadhouse (shown in the drawing) dates from about 1926. However, Jenny King, whose father mined in the Boundary area from about 1935 to 1948, told me the roadhouse was not constructed until the mid 1930s. She said there used to be an older roadhouse at Canyon Creek to the north which may have caused the confusion. In any case, the Boundary Roadhouse is the only surviving building from the community's early days.

After Alaska's purchase from Russia in 1867, the United States government pretty much ignored most of Alaska. Canada, to the contrary, took an active interest in developing the Yukon Territory. According to the book, *Blazing Alaska's Trails*, by Alfred Hulse Brooks, by the time the Klondike Gold Rush started, the Canadian government had already conducted exploratory surveys and preliminary investigations of the Yukon's mineral potential, and the Northwest Mounted Police had established a government and were actively maintaining law and order.

The Canadian government also readily aided miners by building trails and roads, paid for by license fees and taxes on the miners and other local residents. Rather than build the government freight roads along winding creek bottoms, with their muskeg, often impenetrable thickets and hordes of mosquitoes, the Canadians built their main roads and trails along the ridge lines, where the ground was firm, and vegetation was easier to deal with.

Boundary is now accessed via the "Top of The World Highway" (Yukon Highway 9). This 79-mile road, running from Jack Wade Junction on the Taylor Highway to Dawson City, is typical of the roads and trails built by the Canadian government to support the Klondike gold rush.

The highway began in the early 1900s as a government ridge-top pack trail to serve Canadian miners in the Sixty Mile River area and neighboring creeks. The trail was gradually improved and became known as Ridge Road. In the 1920s the ARC in Alaska decided to complete an overland connection to Dawson City by extending its Eagle-Fortymile trail eastwards, and the Canadians obliged by extending their Ridge Road westward.

Winding along the ridge tops, the highway offers beautiful vistas of the Fortymile River drainage to the north. (The Fortymile begins in the U.S. and crosses into Canada before emptying into the Yukon River.) To the south are equally compelling views of the Walker Creek drainage in the U.S., and the Sixty Mile River drainage in Canada.

Sources:

- *A Cultural Resource Inventory of the Fortymile River*. Wendell Bell. U.S. Bureau of Land Management. 1976
- *Blazing Alaska's Trails*. Alfred Hulse Brooks. University of Alaska and the Arctic Institute of North America. 1958
- *Cultural Resource Survey of the Taylor Highway*. Rolfe Buzzell. Alaska Department of Natural Resources. 2003
- Conversation with Jenny King, daughter of Walker Creek miner. 2011
- George King papers, 1915-1969, University of Alaska Fairbanks, Archives. (King was the owner of the Boundary Roadhouse in the 1950s and 60s)
- *Taylor Highway, Fortymile Gold Country, Travel Guide*. BLM. 2007

Alaska Highway, Tanacross

St. Timothy's Church in 2012

Episcopal Church establishes St. Timothy's and Tanacross 100 years ago

2012 marked the 100th anniversary of St. Timothy's Church in Tanacross. The church was one of a string of missions the Episcopal Church established along the Tanana River in the early 1900s to serve the area's Athabascan Indians.

Tanacross is located in Eastern Interior Alaska, about 13 miles west of Tok, just north of the Alaska Highway. When the Episcopal Church decided to start a mission there, Tanacross — then called Tanana Crossing — didn't amount to much. Located along an existing Native trail, which the Eagle-Valdez Trail (blazed in 1899) followed, it was simply a place along the Tanana River shallow enough for horses to ford, and consequently the place where the Eagle-Valdez Trail crossed the river.

A telegraph station, part of the Washington-Alaska Military Cable and Telegraph System, was built there a few years later, as well as a trading post. The telegraph station and trading post were abandoned by 1911. (This is the site where E. T. Barnette wanted to set up his trading post. It seems fortuitous for Barnette that he was forced to disembark at the Chena River instead.)

William Simeone's book, *Rifles, Blankets and Beads: Identity, History, and the Northern Athabaskan Potlatch*, which talks extensively about Tanacross, explains that the Episcopal Church bought the abandoned telegraph station from the federal government. According to early missionary accounts, it took them 20 days to pole a boat upriver from McCarty Station (now called Big Delta State Historical Park) to Tanana Crossing. Arriving on Sept. 25, 1912, the missionaries also appropriated the abandoned trading post and rehabilitated it into the mission.

Although there were no Athabascans living at Tanana Crossing then, there was a sizable village at Mansfield, located about seven miles northwest at Mansfield Lake. It was these people the mission was intended to serve, and they appear to have readily taken to the Christian faith. In the book, *Crow is my Boss*, Tanacross elder Kenny Thomas relates that the people of Mansfield used to walk the seven miles from Mansfield to Tanana Crossing every Sunday to attend church.

One year after the mission was established, gold was discovered in the Chisana River about 95 miles southwest of Tanana Crossing. The Chisana and Nabesna Rivers form the headwaters of the Tanana River, so river traffic bound for the Chisana area had to pass by Tanana Crossing.

This strike attracted hundreds of non-Natives, spurred development of commercial river navigation, and stimulated traders to establish new trading posts along the Tanana River. Several trading ventures were started at Tanana Crossing, and in 1920 a post office was established.

The trading posts and church enticed Natives to start living there at least on a seasonal basis. However, it was not until a Bureau of Indian Affairs school was established in 1932 that Athabascans began settling permanently; moving from Mansfield, Ketchumstuk (30 miles northeast) and other villages. It was also BIA officials who shortened the name of the village from Tanana Crossing to Tanacross in 1934.

The village remained on the Tanana River's north bank until the early 1970s, when water contamination and fears of flooding prompted residents to relocate about a mile away on the south bank of the river. Also, there is no bridge across the Tanana River near the village, and the new location provided road access to the Alaska Highway (constructed in 1942) and the schools and facilities in Tok, only a few miles to the east.

St. Timothy's Church in the new village is a re-creation of the old church, which still stands across the river. Constructed by village residents and dedicated in 1981, the new St. Timothy's is similar in appearance to the old church and even houses the original mission bell.

Sources:

- Conversations with Bruce Grossmann, lay minister at St. Timothy's church; Betty Denny, deacon at St. Timothy's church and daughter of Kenny Thomas Sr.; and Ray Thomas, son of Kenny Thomas Sr.
- *Crow is my Boss, the Oral Life History of a Tanacross Athabaskan Elder*. Kenny Thomas Sr., Edited by Craig Mishler. University of Oklahoma Press. 2005
- *Native and Historic Accounts of some Historic Sites in the Tanacross-Ketchumstock Area*. Elizabeth Andrews. Doyon, LTD. 1980
- *The Eagle-Valdez Trail – Northern Portion*. U.S. Bureau of Land Management. N.D.
- *Rifles, Blankets, & Beads: Identity, History, and the Northern Athapaskan Potlatch*. William Simeone. University of Oklahoma Press. 2002

Dot Lake Community Chapel in 2011

Dot Lake community grew from Alaska Highway construction camp

Dot Lake, located about half way between Tok and Delta Junction on the Alaska Highway, is a picturesque little town on the east shore of Dot Lake. The community did not really exist until the Alaska Highway was constructed, but the area has a long record of aboriginal use. A 2010 archeological excavation at Healy Lake (about 35 miles northwest of Dot Lake) uncovered evidence of human habitation dating to 11,500 years before present.

Athabascan Indians, who have occupied the area for thousands of years, were semi-nomadic. They moved cyclically, depending on the season and availability of resources, and trapped in the Dot Lake area during the winter.

The Tanana River is about ¼ mile to the north, and Dot Lake is on an old Indian freight trail along the river. According to the State of Alaska, by 1924 the Alaska Road Commission (ARC) had built an improved winter trail (called the Tanana Crossing-Grundler Trail) from Big Delta (near present-day Delta Junction) to Tanacross (about 35 miles southeast of Dot Lake). This trail crossed the Tanana River at Sam Creek (about eight miles northwest of the current village site) and probably went by Dot Lake.

When the Alaska Highway was constructed in 1942-43, a construction camp called Sears City was established at Dot Lake. As an interesting aside, most of the Alaska Highway was built by U.S. Army Corps of Engineer troops working side by side with private contractors. However, the section of highway between Tok and Delta Junction was one of the few segments of the highway built solely by a private contractor.

Several of the local Athabascan men worked on the project, and after World War II ended, some Athabascan families began moving to Dot Lake from Sam Lake and Lake George (about 12 miles and 18 miles to the northwest), and from Tanacross. A brochure available at the chapel states that the first Athabascan family to settle at Dot Lake permanently was the Peter Charles family.

Non-Natives also started moving to the area, beginning in 1947 when Fred Vogel acquired several of the cabins used by the Alaska Highway construction crews. It was Vogel who started the lodge at Dot Lake. Stanley Buck, a Christian missionary who also worked for the ARC, began holding services at the Dot Lake lodge at about the same time. Eventually, as the village's population grew, residents decided to build a church. In 1949 a small chapel was constructed on skids next to the lodge and then moved to its present location next to the lake.

By 1952 the community had grown large enough that the Territorial Department of Education was persuaded to send a teacher to Dot Lake. In return for the Territory providing text books and a teacher, the community agreed to construct a school and provide desks.

That first school building sits behind the chapel. The State of Alaska eventually built a new school about a mile away, and for many years the original school building was used as the church parsonage.

With today's paved highway and more fuel efficient vehicles, fewer road travelers stop at Dot Lake than in years past. The gas station is closed, and the former lodge is now a private residence and contract post office. The community is still worth stopping at, though, even if it is just to take photos of the lake (I have seen swans there) and visit the Dot Lake Community Chapel.

Sources:

- *Alaska Community Database.* Alaska Department of Commerce. 2012
- *Annual Report of the Board of Road Commissioners for Alaska.* United States Army. 1917
- *Brief History, Dot Lake Community Chapel.* No author listed. Brochure available at the chapel. No date
- Conversation with Jeff Deeter, present lay leader of the Dot Lake Community Chapel.
- *Dot Lake Socio-Economic Community Profile.* Northwest Alaskan Pipeline Company, 1980
- "Oldest subarctic North American human remains found." Marmian Grimes. UAF Public Affairs news release. 2-24-2011
- *Tanana Crossing-Grundler Trail, RS 2477 Casefile Summary, RST 333.* Alaska, no date Department of Natural Resources
- *Use of Natural Resources by the Residents of Dot Lake, Alaska.* Gayle Martin. Alaska Department of Fish and Game. 1983

Alaska Highway, Delta Junction

Osgood 200 face shovel at Delta Junction

Alcan construction equipment cached in Delta Junction

Many people think that the Alaska Highway ends in Fairbanks. However, most residents of Delta Junction will tell you their hometown is the northern terminus of the highway. (A monument on the bank of the Chena River in downtown Fairbanks used to proclaim Fairbanks as the end of the Alaska Highway, but that signpost was moved to Delta Junction in about 1991.)

Constructed in 1942 as the Alaska Military highway, the road quickly became known as the Alaska-Canadian (Alcan) Highway. According to Harold Richardson's master's thesis, *Building the Alcan Highway: America's Glory Road*, some road crews nicknamed it the "Oilcan Highway" because of all the empty 55-gallon fuel drums scattered along its length. Now it is officially called the Alaska Highway.

A road linking Alaska with Canada and rest of the U.S. had been discussed for many years. In 1933 an Alaska musher, Clyde "Slim" Williams drove his sled and dog team from Alaska to Chicago to help promote such a route. (When the snow ran out in Washington State he put wheels on his sled.)

The 1941 attack on Pearl Harbor, and perceived Japanese threat in the Northern Pacific and Alaska spurred development, though. President Roosevelt approved the project on February 11, 1942, and work began later that spring.

In order to speed construction, the project was begun at multiple locations along the proposed route. Construction crews began working north from Dawson Creek in British Columbia, east and west from the Whitehorse area in the Yukon Territory, and east from Big Delta (now Delta Junction) in Alaska.

The original plan called for U.S. Army Corps of Engineers personnel to punch through a pioneer road, followed by civilian contractors who would build a standard road using the pioneer road for access. However, it quickly became apparent this was unrealistic (at least in terms of getting the road built in one construction season).

Consequently, civilian contractors worked alongside army personnel, improving the pioneer road so military convoys could safely use it. By the time the road was competed in November 1942, 11,000 troops and 7,500 civilians had worked on the highway.

A small cache of equipment and vehicles used during highway construction can be seen at Delta Junction. The equipment is located between the Delta Junction Visitor Center and the Sullivan Roadhouse Museum, and includes an Osgood 200 face shovel, Caterpillar D8 bulldozer with Letourneau ripper, Studebaker US6 6x6 cargo truck, and several other vehicles. (The Osgood excavator is shown in the drawing.) Much of the equipment was donated by local residents.

When I talked with Jeff McNabb, a Delta resident who was involved with acquiring and moving the equipment, he said the site itself is another remnant of World War II history. The property was once a transfer point for the CANOL Pipeline, a project to supply fuel for the Alaska Highway and Northern Staging Route (a series of airfields, through which military aircraft were ferried from the U.S. to the Soviet Union.) At Big Delta, a stub line went south to supply fuel to the Big Delta Army Airfield (now Fort Greely).

The Alaska Highway has been straightened and improved over the years. There are just a few spots left where you can see or experience the original road. The equipment at Delta Junction is one of the only places in Alaska where you can still touch a piece of Alcan history.

Sources:

- "Building the Alcan Highway, America's Glory Road." Harold Richardson. Master's thesis, University of Colorado. 1943
- Conversation with Jeff McNabb, Delta resident involved in acquiring and moving equipment
- *The Alaska Highway*. Jane Haigh. Wolf Creek Books. 2000
- *The Earthmover Encyclopedia: The Complete Guide to Heavy Equipment of the World.* Keith Haddock. Motorbooks International. 2003
- *The Forgotten War – Volume One.* Stan Cohen. Pictorial Histories Publishing Company. 1981
- *Trail of '42.* Stan Cohen, Pictorial Histories Publishing Company. 1979

Richardson Highway, Black Rapids

Black Rapids Roadhouse in 2011

Historic roadhouse at Black Rapids escapes destruction

Roadhouses were essential in Alaska during the early historical period. Situated a day's travel apart (about 25 miles) along main trails they provided shelter and food for travelers, and often served as community centers. As trails and roads improved or were re-routed, some roadhouses fell into disuse. With the introduction of automobiles people could travel further in a day, and more roadhouses were abandoned or converted to other uses.

There used to be about 30 roadhouses along the Valdez-Fairbanks Trail (Richardson Highway). Now only a handful are left. One of those is Black Rapids Roadhouse (shown in the drawing) about 40 miles south of Delta

Junction. It is right across the highway from the Delta River and Black Rapids glacier.

The roadhouse opened around 1904, and was added onto Alaska-fashion over the years. It appears the oldest part of the roadhouse (the two-story log section at the south end) began as a single story, and the second floor was added later. Sections were gradually added to the north, south and east.

By the 1990s it was a rambling structure, and like an ancient English manor house, parts of it had fallen into decay. The roadhouse finally closed in 1993 and by the end of the decade it appeared destined for total collapse. Several of the additions had already collapsed, the roof on the center section was caving in and the two-story portion was propped upright with poles.

In 1999, Annie and Michael Hopper bought the property, planning to build a lodge (the new *Lodge at Black Rapids*) on the ridge behind the decaying roadhouse. Convinced the old roadhouse could be saved, the couple undertook restoring the roadhouse as well as building a new lodge.

After getting the structure added to the National Register of Historic Places and obtaining some grant funding, they (assisted by a small group of dedicated volunteers) tore down irreparable portions of the structure, and set about stabilizing the roadhouse's oldest section.

After carefully raising the structure in sections, they put in concrete footings and new bottom courses of treated timbers. Salvaged or new logs replaced damaged ones and roofing was repaired. Now the building looks about like it did in 1915. The Hoppers hope to rebuild additional portions of the roadhouse with salvaged materials, finish the restoration, and eventually open it as a museum.

Of course, if the Black Rapids Glacier had its way, there might not be a roadhouse to restore. Back in 1937 the glacier, which now sits far up the valley across the river, surged forward, threatening to overrun the Delta River, Richardson Highway, and roadhouse. Experts estimated that the glacier traveled 220 feet per day. Between December 3, 1936 and March 7, 1937 it covered about four miles.

The mile and a quarter face of the glacier stopped just short of the Delta River. If the glacier had overrun the river, it wouldn't have been the first time. Geologic evidence points to another surge about 600 years ago that dammed the river. The Trans-Alaska Oil Pipeline runs along the base of the mountains behind the new lodge, and engineers were very concerned about possible threats to the pipeline from the glacier. Fortunately for the old roadhouse, new lodge and pipeline, scientists think a repeat of the galloping glacier is unlikely any time soon.

Sources:

- "Black Rapids Glacier Galloped to Fame in 1937." Ned Rozell. Alaska Science Forum, article #1342. June 19, 1997
- "Black Rapids Roadhouse Restoration Project." Michael Hopper. The Lodge at Black Rapids website. No date
- Conversation with Michael Hopper, owner of Black Rapids Lodge
- *Roadhouses of the Richardson Highway*. Walter Phillips. Alaska Historical Commission. 1985
- *The Trail, the Story of the Historic Valdez-Fairbanks Trail*. Kenneth Marsh. Trapper Creek Museum. 2008

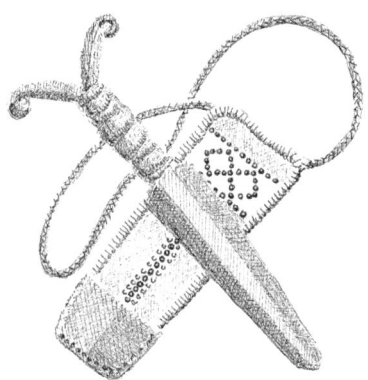

Richardson Highway, Delta Junction

WAMCATS station at Big Delta in 2009

Big Delta WAMCATS station helped link Fairbanks to the world

Issues of Fairbanks newspapers from the 1910s often printed ads for businesses announcing goods soon to be arriving from Valdez over the Valdez-Fairbanks Trail. How did Fairbanks businesses, isolated in Interior Alaska 360 miles away from Valdez, know when something was coming?

Turns out that running parallel to parts of the trail were telegraph lines—a segment of the Washington-Alaska Military Cable and Telegraph System (WAMCATS). Cargo lists for stages could be telegraphed from Valdez, and travelers had access to the line at telegraph stations about 20-30 miles apart along the trail (often near roadhouses). Indeed, from its earliest days, Fairbanks, though physically isolated, was connected to the outside world by telegraph.

The U.S. government, spurred by the Klondike gold rush, had established Army posts across Alaska at the close of the 1890s, including Fort Davis at Nome, Fort St. Michael near the mouth of the Yukon River, Fort Gibbon at Tanana on the Middle Yukon, Fort Egbert at Eagle (six miles from Canadian border) and Fort Liscum at Valdez. In 1900 the U.S. Army Signal Corps began constructing a telegraph system to link those posts with each other and the contiguous United States.

Amazingly, the entire system was completed and operating within five years. A link with the rest of the world was actually established by 1901 when a line was run from Fort Egbert at Eagle to Dawson City in Canada. (Canadian authorities had already strung telegraph lines from Dawson City and Whitehorse to British Columbia.) The U.S. however, wanted an "All-American" system, so submarine cables were eventually laid from Valdez to Southeast Alaska and Seattle.

The system, as completed in 1904, included 1,439 miles of land lines, a 107-mile wireless link across Norton Sound, and 2,079 miles of submarine cable. Congress judiciously planned for civilian as well as military use of the new system and by 1906 about 80 percent of all messages sent across the government wires were civilian in nature.

A telegraph line to Fairbanks wasn't included in the original plans. The telegraph line from Fort St. Michael would have followed the Yukon River most of the way to Eagle, but Felix Pedro's 1902 gold discovery changed that. The line from St. Michael was diverted at Tanana and quickly extended along the Tanana River (with a slight detour to Fairbanks) to link up with the WAMCATS Eagle-Valdez section.

The telegraph station at McCarty (now called Big Delta and Rika's Roadhouse) is shown in the drawing. McCarty Station was built in 1906-07 to replace the Goodpaster Station which was destoyed by fire. It originally consisted of at least four log structures containing the telegraph office, living quarters and warehouse space. Several of those buildings have been restored and are now part of Big Delta State Historical Park.

The building pictured was originally a storehouse, but has been outfitted to reflect the life of early telegraph operators. According to a National Register of Historic Places document, while the structure may appear to be two cabins that were joined together, evidence suggests the entire building was built at one time utilizing short logs.

WAMCATS landlines, because of harsh winters and poor soil conditions, were extremely hard to maintain, and as sections wore out they were replaced by less expensive, more dependable and more easily maintained wireless telegraph (radio) communications. All the telegraph stations that supported land-lines had closed by 1925 but McCarty received a 50 watt radio in 1926 which was in operation until 1935. That same year the WAMCATS buildings were transferred to the Alaska Road Commission (ARC).

With the switch from telegraph to radio, WAMCATS was renamed the Alaska Communications System (ACS), still under Army control. ACS wended it way from Army to Air Force control and eventually to private ownership. As a private corporation it was renamed Alascom and is now part of AT&T.

Sources:

- *Alaska Community Database*, Alaska Department of Community and Regional Affairs, 2011
- *Big Delta State Historical Park*. Alaska Department of Natural Resource. No date
- "Big Delta Historic District National Register of Historic Places Registration Form." Janet F. Clemens, U.S. Park Service, 1990
- "Communications," chapter 4-13 of *Alaska's Heritage*. Alaska Humanities Forum website. 2004
- *Eagle – Fort Egbert, a Remnant of the Past*. U.S. Bureau of Land Management. 2008

Richardson Highway, Richardson

The Haines homestead in 2012

John Haines homestead still provides inspiration

Here is the place I came to,
the lost bridge, my camp
made of shouldered boards
nailed to this hill, by a road
surveyed out of nowhere.

A door blows aside in the wind,
and a path worn deep to the spring
showers familiar leaves.

A battered dipper shines here
in the dusk; the trees stand close,
their branches are moving,
In flight with the rustling of wings...

(From the poem "Homestead" in *News from the Glacier*, 1982)

Seventy miles southwest of Fairbanks, near Richardson, lies the homestead that birthed poet and essayist John Meade Haines. Not physically of course — he was 23 years old when he came to Alaska — but metaphorically. Over several decades, it was that homestead and the country around it that shaped much of his writing. In his poem, "Homestead," he wrote, "The land gave up its meaning slowly, as the sun finds day by day, a deeper place in the mountain."

John Haines was not a prolific writer, but he was a sublime poet and essayist. Haines' writings, at least in his early years in Alaska, were rooted in the earth. His poems and essays are often deeply introspective and filled with haunting imagery of the wilderness around him and the few humans who shared it.

In addition to numerous other honors he received, he was a former Port Laureate of Alaska and was awarded two Guggenheim Fellowships, a National Endowment for the Arts Fellowship and a Lifetime Achievement Award from the Library of Congress.

Trained as an artist, Haines drove to Alaska in 1947, hoping to make his career as a painter. He bought a 160-acre homestead on a hillside above the Tanana River near Richardson and set about building a home.

An abandoned section of the Richardson Highway ran through his homestead, as did Gasoline Creek (so named because Richardson was one of the few places along the highway where motorists could obtain fuel). On the advice of a local sourdough, Haines salvaged planking and squared timbers from an old bridge across the creek, and built a 12-foot by 16-foot frame cabin a few hundred feet away along the down-slope edge of the abandoned right-of-way. A south-facing window-filled wannigan, and enclosed entry to the east were added later.

Eventually, a string of buildings (including an old trapper's cabin moved from Banner Creek) lined the edge of the road. The trapper's cabin served as his workshop, and an outhouse and several storage sheds completed the lineup. On the up-slope side of the road were his garden plot and greenhouse. Dan O'Neill, a friend of Haines, told me that poet William Stafford, also one of John's friends, once said John's little assemblage of buildings looked "like a train coming around the curve."

Although Haines moved to Alaska as a painter, he eventually abandoned art (when as he says, his paints froze) and took up writing. That hardly paid any bills during his early years in Alaska, so he earnestly lived the life of a homesteader — gardening, hunting, trapping, fishing and working odd jobs. It is from these experiences on the homestead that much of his writing sprang.

His success as a writer allowed him to step away from some of the duties of a homesteader, and he eventually built a small writing studio uphill from his cabin. In 1969 he sold the homestead, moving to the Lower 48. He returned to Alaska years later, living at the old homestead for a time before moving to Anchorage and then Fairbanks. He died in Fairbanks in March 2011.

On top of the ridge above his cabin there is a bench in a small south-facing clearing where Haines would sit and ponder, gazing out over the Tanana River Valley. It is here that some of his friends gathered in the summer of 2012 to scatter his ashes. Attached to a stone near the bench is a memorial plaque with a single line from his essay, "Spring." It reads simply "Be still, like a stone in the sun."

Sources:

- Conversation with Dan O'Neill, long-time friend of John Haines
- *The Owl in the Mask of the Dreamer*. Collected poems by John Haines. Graywolf Press. 1993,
- "The Poetry of John Haines" (introduction to *New Poems: 1980-1988*). Edited by Dana Gioia. Story Line Press. 1990
- *The Stars, the Snow, the Fire: Twenty-five Years in the Alaska Wilderness*, John Haines, Graywolf Press. 1989

Richardson Highway, Richardson

Richardson Roadhouse in 1990

Little remains of Richardson Roadhouse and community around it

When I moved to Fairbanks in 1983, Richardson (about 70 miles to the southeast) was a pale shadow of its former self. By the 80s all that was left were a few year-round and seasonal residences, a scattering of abandoned cabins, and the remains of the Richardson Roadhouse (shown in the drawing).

However, in 1907 the town boasted 500 residents, a roadhouse, grocery store, post office and telegraph station. Gold had been discovered along Tenderfoot Creek in 1905, resulting in a minor stampede to the northwest on Banner and other nearby creeks. A score of drift mines were developed in the area, and since small steamboats could reach

Banner Creek on the Tanana River, a town quickly sprang up there.

It was also along the Fairbanks-Valdez Trail, and the town was named in honor of Wilds P. Richardson, head of the Alaska Road Commission. Richardson was the supply center for nearby creeks and the town's early prospects seemed promising. The Tanana Valley Railroad even planned an extension to the area, but the amount of gold in the creeks proved low and those plans were abandoned. Just as elsewhere, when the larger paystreaks played out, Richardson's fortune's plummeted.

The Tanana River changed course in 1915, encroaching on Richardson and forcing the town to move about a mile north, away from the river. That was when the telegraph station closed. Again in the mid-1920s the town was faced by an angry river, and again it moved north. Each time Richardson moved, it was a smaller town. Eventually all that remained were a few hardened miners, some trappers and homesteaders, and the people at the roadhouse.

Richardson has hosted three roadhouses. The remains you can see today are of the third one, started by Fred Wilkins in about 1915. He homesteaded in the area and ran Richardson's general store. When the town relocated in the 1920s, Wilkins moved his operation to the north side of the highway. His roadhouse eventually became known as Richardson Roadhouse.

For decades the roadhouse served highway travelers and the dwindling population of Richardson. John Haines, poet and essayist, lived on a Richardson homestead for years. He mentions the roadhouse often — of sitting at tables listening to old-timers' stories, of community gatherings there on Thanksgiving and Christmas, and of watching as the area's history silently slipped away.

In his essay "Mudding Up," Haines wrote that "this quiet, rural world of Richardson, with its few surviving people and its old-fashioned implements, remote and settled on a stretch of gravel road, was vanishing even as I came to know it."

By 1980 the roadhouse consisted of a one-story log café with false front, a small motel unit and a log garage with two associated small wood-frame buildings. The cafe was destroyed by fire in 1982 but the garage operated a few years more.

The roadhouse was closed and vacant by the 1990s, the gas pumps pulled up. In July of 2011 the owners, plagued by persistent vandalism, tore down the motel unit and the two small wood-frame buildings. Little remains except the old log garage and a sign obscured by encroaching trees.

Sources:

- Conversation with Eileen Brado, Fairbanks North Star Borough Property Appraiser
- Fairbanks North Star Borough property records
- *Historic Resources in the Fairbanks North Star Borough*. Janet Matheson & F. Bruce Haldeman. Fairbanks North Star Borough. 1981
- *Roadhouses of the Richardson Highway*. Walter Phillips. Alaska Historical Commission. 1984
- *The Stars, the Snow, the Fire: Twenty-Five Years in the Alaska Wilderness*. John Haines. Graywolf Press. 1989
- *The Trail, the Story of the Historic Valdez-Fairbanks Trail*. Kenneth Marsh. Trapper Creek Museum. 2008

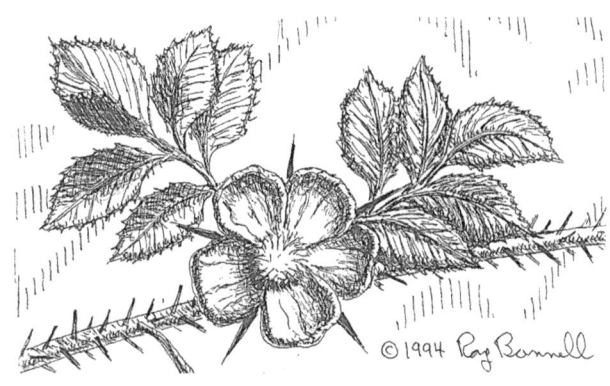

Richardson Highway, Munson's Slough

Salchaket Native cemetery in 1995

Salcha Native Cemetery, a people and place worth remembering

A few miles northwest of the Salcha River bridge on the Richardson Highway is a small cemetery perched on the bluff overlooking Munson's Slough and the Tanana River. The picturesque Salcha Native Cemetery, only a short distance from where the native village used to be, is one of the last vestiges of the Salcha band (also called Salchaket) of Tanana Athabaskan Indians.

According to Elizabeth Andrews' 1975 Master's thesis about the Salchaket, the people actually called themselves Saacaege. This term means "the mouth of the Salcha River," but was used to refer to the people and location. Salchaket is an English corruption of Saacaege.

Among the Tanana Athabascans, bands were the primary social unit beyond family. These bands were semi-nomadic, with each one normally having a central winter camp and several seasonal hunting and fishing camps. They moved cyclically, depending on the season and availability of resources. The region's primary villages were located near the best fishing and hunting areas, usually on clear water tributaries of the Tanana River or near larger lakes.

The Salcha River, second-largest tributary of the Tanana River, is a salmon spawning stream and the Salchaket main village was located at its confluence with the Tanana River. It was here in 1898 that A. H. Brooks (with the U.S. Geological Survey) made the first recorded contact with Salcha natives.

Interaction between the Salcha band and Westerners was limited before the Klondike Gold Rush(1897). Shortly after 1900 Westerners began moving into the area.

In 1902 the U.S. Army Signal Corps constructed a telegraph station several miles upriver from the native village. Prospectors discovered gold on several tributaries of the Salcha River, and in 1904 William F. Munson established Munson's Roadhouse near the village to supply the miners and other local residents. The Alaska Road Commission (ARC) completed a winter trail between Valdez and Fairbanks (which passed near the Salcha telegraph station) in 1907 and a summer wagon trail by 1910.

St. Luke's Episcopal mission opened at the native village in 1909, the same year that a post office was established. By 1911 there were about 40 natives living there. The mission closed in 1920, and during the mid 1920s the community lost its post office and the telegraph station. By the late 1920s the community's population had dwindled to about 25 people. The area's native population continued to shrink and by the 1940s only a handful of Indians remained.

Before the Episcopal mission's demise, the native cemetery was established. A 1914 Episcopal publication wrote of the cemetery being started after the death of the village's chief Jarvis. Aside from that little is known about the cemetery's history. There are only seven graves there, most of them old, with spruce growing up in their midst. Several have picket fences. The most recent grave dates to 1988, when Bessie Barnabus, one of the last Salchakets familiar with the traditional way of life was buried there. Her family estimated that she was over 100 when she died.

The bluff is a peaceful location with a lovely view of the Tanana River. I enjoy watching chickadees and I drew the cemetery in late winter, after the birch catkins had dropped their winter seeds. I hope that Bessie Barnabus is at peace with chickadees dancing on her grave.

Sources:

- *A Handbook of the Church's Mission to the Indians*. No author listed, Episcopal Church Missions Publishing Company. 1913
- Conversation with Bob Sattler, archaeologist with Tanana Chiefs Conference
- *Early Transportation Routes, Fort Wainwright*. Ronald Neely. Center for Environmental Management of Military Lands. 2003
- "Not Forgotten - Borough working to preserve historic burial site." Kate Ripley. *Fairbanks Daily News-Miner.* September 21, 1997
- *Historic Resources in the Fairbanks North Star Borough.* Janet Matheson & F. Bruce Haldeman. Fairbanks North Star Borough. 1981
- "Salcha: an Athabascan band of the Tanana River and its culture.." Elizabeth Andrews. Master's thesis, University of Alaska Fairbanks. 1975
- "Salcha River Navigability Report." U.S. Bureau of Land Management. 2005
- *The Alaska Churchman*, Guy Madara. Episcopal Church of Alaska. November 1914

Denali Highway, Valdez Creek

Valdez Creek post office in 2000

Log cabin post office one of few buildings left along Valdez Creek

The road from the Denali Highway to Valdez Creek, about 60 miles east of Cantwell, is rough even on a nice day. The day I drove in, heavy rain had partially washed out several culverts. Fortunately miners still work local creeks and by the time I drove back out the road was repaired.

When I arrived at Valdez Creek and the old mining camp of Denali, the first sight to greet me was the small log cabin shown in the drawing, built by miner Leburn Wickersham in the early 1900s. It is one of the last buildings at the settlement, and served as Denali's post office until 1942.

Valdez Creek is a tributary of the Susitna River and tumbles down out of the Clearwater Mountains. At the end of the 19th century, this region was one of the few Alaska areas still unexplored by Westerners. The Bureau of Land

Management (BLM) report, *An Historical Resource Study of the Valdez Creek Mining District*, records that a group of prospectors from Cook Inlet finally reached the Susitna's headwaters in 1897.

Working their way upriver, they panned numerous creeks—finding little gold until reaching what is now called Valdez Creek. By then their eyes were so swollen from mosquito bites they named the swiftly flowing stream "Swollen Creek." Placer gold appeared relatively abundant, but they lacked equipment for serious development, and low supplies forced them to return to Cook Inlet. Word of their discovery spread but it wasn't until 1903 that their creek was "re-discovered."

In February of 1903 a party of men led by prospector Peter Monahan (veteran of both the Klondike and Nome gold rushes) left Valdez, mushing north over the Valdez Glacier Trail to prospect in Copper River country. They spent six months working along the eastern edge of the Talkeetna Mountains and eventually shifted westward into the Susitna River drainage.

In August Monahan's party struck paydirt on the same creek the 1897 prospectors had discovered. They staked and worked claims until September, returning to Valdez with several hundred ounces of gold. Monahan renamed the stream, "Valdez Creek," in honor of his home-base.

When Monahan and partners returned the next year, hundreds of eager gold seekers trailed them. Soon the majority of creeks in the area were staked, and a haphazard little settlement sprang up. Valdez Creek is in a remote, mountainous area, and most of the miners weren't interested in toughing out the long harsh winters. Few permanent structures were erected, and those were scattered across the hills.

At first the settlement was called "Galina," the English equivalent of an Ahtna Athabascan word meaning "place where game abounds." Ahtna had lived in the area for generations and Valdez Creek was one of their main hunting areas in the Upper Susitna region—the site of a seasonal hunting camp.

The settlement was later called McKinley and eventually Denali. By the summer of 1908 there were 180 residents, but only about 20 lived there year-round.

Actually, according to an article in the Fall 2003 issue of *BLM Alaska Frontiers*, two settlements developed. A white community was located on Valdez Creek's west bank, and an Ahtna village sprang up about a mile to the east.

Many of Valdez Creek's Native residents came from villages in the Tyone River area about 50 miles south southeast of the Clearwater Mountains. Valdez Creek was within their territory, and they provided fish and game for the miners as well as working a few of the mines.

Denali's heyday (at least in terms of population) only lasted a few years. The really rich paystreaks were hundreds of feet underground and most miners moved on after a few years. Large companies later developed those deep deposits, but most of the settlement's old buildings were demolished in the process. Today all that is left is a small cemetery and few scattered cabins.

Sources:

- *An Historical Resource Study of the Valdez Creek Mining District—Alaska*. Peter F. Dessauer & David W. Harvey. U.S. Bureau of Land Management. 1980
- *Denali Mine on Valdez Creek, South Central Alaska: A Cultural Resources Evaluation.* Beth E. Walton & Cheryl A. McCaffrey. BLM. 1984
- *Dictionary of Alaska Place Names, Geological Survey professional paper 567*. Donald J. Orth. U.S. Geological Survey. 1971
- "The Valdez Creek Mining District, Alaska in 1936," in *Mineral Resources of Alaska*. Ralph Tuck. U.S. Geological Survey. 1936
- "Valdez Creek quietly turns 100," in *BLM Alaska Frontiers*. Robert King. BLM. Fall 2003

Denali National Park and Preserve, Headquarters Site

Dog feed cache in 2011

Denali National Park dog feed cache reflects park's mushing history

Dog mushing has been an important activity in the Denali region since before the establishment of Mount McKinley National Park (now Denali National Park and Preserve). Ahtna Indians indigenous to the area traditionally used dog teams for transport, and when Charles Alexander Sheldon (the father of Denali National Park) spent the winter of 1907-08 studying wildlife near the headwaters of the Toklat River, he and his packer, Harry Karstens, used dog teams extensively.

Karstens, an 1897 Klondike veteran, was an experienced sourdough. (He was the guide for the first successful ascent of Mount McKinley in 1913.) Although the park was established in 1917, it languished for several years because Congress failed to provide funding. However, in 1921 funds were finally appropriated (partly because of the imminent completion of the Alaska Railroad through the area) and Harry Karstens was appointed the new park's superintendent (and only employee).

It was Karstens who chose the park's entrance at Riley Creek and of necessity hastily built a headquarters area just west of the nearly completed Alaska Railroad. According to a National Park Service document, *Historic Resource Study of Denali National Park and Preserve*, having the park headquarters in the low-lying creek bottom next to the railroad was less than ideal. Karstens moved his headquarters to its present upland location along the Park road between Rock and Hines Creeks in 1925.

One of Karstens' first priorities was to bring the rampant poaching along the park's northern boundary under control. Mount McKinley National Park had been established in part to protect the region's wildlife, but commercial hunters routinely ignored the park boundaries to obtain meat for Fairbanks and other Interior communities. Karstens established the park's first kennel to provide reliable sled dogs for patrolling the park's wilderness.

A dog feed cache that combined workshop, food storage and food preparation areas, was constructed in about 1929. It was built in the "Rustic Style," which attempted to harmonize with the surrounding environment and used local building traditions and materials.

Constructed with a peeled log frame, and reverse board and batten siding (wide boards on the outside, thin boards inside covering gaps between wide boards), it was one and a half stories high, and originally consisted of just the central room with storage above, and a smaller food prep room adjacent (to the left in the drawing). Karstens' grandson, Ken, told me that preparing food in the new building was a vast improvement over the old method—cooking the food in a huge copper kettle inside a surplus railroad construction tent (and stirring the pot with an oar).

The structure was moved by the Civilian Conservation Corps in 1938 to its present location at the top of a steep slope above Hines Creek. In 1976 a sled storage room was added (to the right in the drawing). Over the years there have been other minor changes or additions. (For instance, the upper storage room was originally accessed by climbing a ladder.) The building is now part of the park's Headquarters Historic District.

Dog mushing, and consequently, the park's dog kennels, have continued to be important assets in managing the park. They provide a link with Denali National Park's history and allow winter access into the park's original 2-million acre parcel, which is now designated as wilderness.

The Park Service maintains about 30 huskies at the kennels. During the winter the dogs provide transportation for rangers, collectively logging about 3,000 miles. In the summer the huskies are the center of the park's most popular interpretive program, daily sled dog demonstrations that attract over 50,000 people annually.

Sources:

- Correspondence with Ken Karstens (Harry Karstens' grandson). 2011
- *A History of Mt. McKinley National Park*. Grant Peterson. National Park Service. 1953
- "Denali National Park Sled Dog Kennel." Denali National Park and Preserve website. 2011
- "Dog Feed Cache and Sled Storage Building." Sandra Faulkner. Historic American Buildings Survey. 1986
- *Historic Resource Study of Denali National Park and Preserve, Volume 1 - Historical Narrative*. William Brown. National Park Service. 1991
- *Land Use in the North Additions of Denali National Park and Preserve: a Historical perspective*. William Schneider, Dianne Gudgel-Holmes and John Dalle-Molle. National Park Service. 1984

Denali National Park and Preserve, Kantishna

Busia cabin in 1995

Kantishna's Busia cabin exudes Alaskan ambiance

Nestled at the base of tundra-covered mountains in Kantishna sits the small log cabin pictured in the drawing. According to National Park Service records it was built in 1922. This cabin, with its moose antlers over the door and traps hanging on the wall, looks quintessentially Alaskan to me.

You could also say that the man who lived there, Johnny Busia (pronounced boo-shay), was a quintessential Alaskan sourdough — a miner and trapper who spent over 40 years in the Kantishna area. In his later years, when Busia was Kantishna's sole year-round resident, Park Service employees affectionately called him the town's unofficial mayor. He died there in 1957 and the mountain behind Busia's cabin is named in his honor.

Kantishna (originally called Eureka) is a tiny isolated hamlet located north of Mount McKinley. Situated at the confluence of Eureka and Moose Creeks and three miles northwest of Wonder Lake, the community is 95 road-miles west of the Parks Highway and about as far west as you can travel by vehicle and still be connected to the U.S. continental road system. The hills and ridges are covered by alpine tundra, and the valleys by taiga forest.

Tom Walker's book, *Kantishna Mushers, Miners, Mountaineers*, relates that hundreds, perhaps thousands of gold seekers flooded the Kantishna Hills in late 1905 after Joe Quigley, Jack Horn, Joe Dalton and Simon Stiles brought news to Fairbanks of rich diggings in the area. Several mining camps quickly sprang up. Kantishna was near the best placer deposits, but miles by rough trails from major transportation points. Other towns, such as Diamond and Glacier City, were established at the upstream limits of navigability on local rivers.

Unfortunately, the "sunburnt" gold (lying close to the surface) concentrated in only a few creeks and was soon exhausted. The boom ended within six months. Most miners abandoned their claims, and communities became ghost towns almost overnight. By the summer of 1906 Kantishna, being closest to the rich diggings, was the sole surviving town, and only a few score of hardy miners remained. Even then it was only a summer town. Few of the miners stuck it out during the long harsh winters.

Johnny, a Croatian immigrant, came to Kantishna in 1918 to join his father and uncle. The cabin in the drawing, built by the Kantishna Hydraulic Mining Company, was abandoned when Johnnie moved into it in 1922 or 1923.

The fortunes of Kantishna have ebbed and surged several times, but the town has always remained small, in part due to its remoteness and the difficulties shipping supplies in and ore out. Mount McKinley National Park was established just to the south in 1917, and when the park boundaries were expanded in 1980 the new park addition completely enveloped the private lands at Kantishna. Five years later all commercial mining activity within the park boundaries was indefinitely halted by court order.

Much of the private property around Kantishna, including Busia's cabin, has been acquired by the National Park Service. A 2008 National Park Service planning document highlighted restoration work on the cabin, including replacing windows, doors, roof, and some logs. The moose antlers and traps are gone, but the building still exudes Alaskan ambiance. Other inholdings were bought by backcountry lodges, and Kantishna is now a magnet for tourists.

Since Kantishna's inception, the mountaineers, hunters and other adventurers roaming the northern flanks of the Alaska Range have been drawn by the area's natural wonders and have raved over the hospitality of Kantishna's residents. That part of the Kantishna spirit lives on even today.

Sources:

- *A History of Mt. McKinley National Park*, Grant Peterson. National Park Service. 1953
- *Denali National Park and Preserve Resource Stewardship Strategy 2008 – 2027 Summary*. National Park Service. 2008
- *Historic Resource Study of Denali National Park and Preserve, Volume 1 - Historical Narrative*. William Brown. National Park Service. 1991
- "Johnnie Busia, Mayor of Kantishna," in *Denali History Nuggets*. Erik Johnson. National Park Service. 2018
- *Kantishna Mushers, Miners, Mountaineers: the Story behind Mt. McKinley National Park*. Tom Walker. Pictorial Histories Publishing Company. 2005
- *Land Use in the North Additions of Denali National Park and Preserve: a Historical perspective*. William Schneider, Dianne Gudgel-Holmes and John Dalle-Molle. National Park Service. 1984
- "Going for Gold in Kantishna," in *Alaska Park Journal*. Vol. 5, Issue 2. Ann Kain & Phil Breaze. National Park Service. 2006

Parks Highway, Healy

Healy Hotel (now Princess Tours employee housing) in 2013

Historic Healy Hotel lives on at new location

Most people driving the Parks Highway through Healy have no idea they can see a historic structure from the road. However, the two-story building just to the north and east of the Healy Spur Road intersection used to be the historic Healy Hotel.

Healy began as a mining and hunting camp in about 1904, during the same period when gold prospectors made strikes at Kantishna, 70 miles to the southwest; and Bonnifield, 40 miles to the northeast. Prospectors used to ascend into the mountains east of the Nenana River via a trail up Healy Creek, a tributary of the Nenana located across the river from the present townsite.

According to William Brown's book, *Historic Resource Study of Denali National Park and Preserve*, a roadhouse and store were established on the bluff across from Healy Creek, and commercial hunters also used the site as a base of operations. This early camp was sometimes called Dry Creek and sometimes Healy Fork.

Outcroppings of coal are common in the area. The Alaska Department of Natural Resources reports that geologists in the early 1900s estimated the area contained about 10 billion tons of coal reserve. Of course, there was no way to get that coal to market, and early residents only mined the easily accessible seams for local use.

Construction of the Alaska Railroad changed all that. The railroad follows the Nenana River from Broad Pass to the Tanana River, and the Alaska Engineering Commission (AEC - tasked with building the railroad) built a construction camp at Healy Forks. By the end of the 1910s the AEC had built a hotel to house train crews and visiting railroad employees, dormitory, mess hall, hospital, warehouse, blacksmith shop, and other facilities.

The Alaska Railroad also spurred development of coal mining in the area. Beginning in 1918, several small coal mines were opened along the Nenana River, along Lignite Creek just to the North of Healy, and at Suntrana Creek, about 2.5 miles up Healy Creek. These coal mines found ready customers in Fairbanks, where wood cutting had denuded the hills for miles around the city, and the newly organized Fairbanks Exploration Company needed inexpensive and dependable power to provide electricity for its fleet of gold dredges.

After World War II the townsite of Healy moved about a half mile to the north. This was in part because the old hotel had burned down, but also because river erosion was threatening the community. A new hotel was built in 1946. A flat-roofed two-story wood-frame structure, it was similar in appearance to the depot next door.

Suntrana developed into its own little company town, but was eventually absorbed by the Usibelli Company, which began mining coal in the Healy area in 1943. Usibelli continued to house workers at Suntrana until the 1970s, when expansion of coal mining nearby forced the company to find alternative employee housing.

Construction of the Parks Highway (connecting Anchorage and Fairbanks) had been completed in 1972, and the community immediately began gravitating towards the highway. In 1978 Usibelli leased a large land tract near the highway from the Alaska Railroad, subdivided it, and subleased lots to its employees. Suntrana was abandoned and Healy grew.

Changing social and economic conditions led the railroad to close many of its Healy facilities, including the hotel. In her book, *Buildings of Alaska*, Alison Hoagland writes that the hotel building was sold to private investors. In 1986 it was moved to its present location next to the Parks Highway and placed on a new full basement. Aside from new siding and a pitched roof, the old hotel, which now houses Princess Tours employees, looks much the same as it did when railroad crews called it home.

Sources:

- *Buildings of Alaska*. Alison K. Hoagland. Oxford University Press. 1993
- Denali Borough land records
- "Healy Creek Trail, RS 2477 Casefile Summary, RST 444." Alaska Department of Natural Resources. No date
- *Historic Resource Study of Denali National Park and Preserve, Volume 1 - Historical Narrative*. William Brown. National Park Service. 1991
- *Mining the Burning Hills: a History of Alaska's Suntrana Coal Mine and Townsite*. Rolfe G. Buzzell. Alaska Department of Natural Resources, 1994
- Photos of Healy Hotel in 1952, from James Ava Collection. AlaskaRails.Org website

Parks Highway, Nenana

St. Mark's Church in 2011

St. Mark's Episcopal Church a reminder of Nenana's early history

Traveling through the small town of Nenana, about 60 miles south of Fairbanks, you might get the impression that it is a relatively new community—the fortuitous juncture of the Alaska Railroad, Parks Highway and Tanana River. However, the area has been occupied for a much longer period of time.

According to a 1984 report done for the Alaska Department of Fish and Game, Athabascan Indians were living near the confluence of the Tanana and Nenana Rivers on a seasonal basis hundreds of years before non-Natives discovered the site. It was a gathering place where Indians came for mid-winter potlatches and summer fishing. Natives called the village Toghotthele (meaning "mountain that parallels the river"), but early western explorers corrupted that to Tortella. Now the town is called Nenana after the nearby river.

The original village was two miles up the Tanana and across the river from Nenana's present location. In 1900, when non-Natives began pushing into the Tanana basin, the village featured about 20 cabins. A telegraph station was established in the village in 1902, and the next year a trading post was built there.

The Episcopal Church, continuing work done by Episcopal and Anglican missionaries along the Yukon River, envisioned a series of missions throughout the Tanana basin to serve its Native population. Eventually four missions were established: St. Barnabas at Chena Native Village (about two miles below the confluence of the Chena and Tanana Rivers), St. Luke's at Salcha, St. Timothy's at Tanacross (near Tok), and St. Mark's at Nenana. The churches at Chena Native Village and Salcha eventually closed, but those at Tanacross and Nenana still survive.

Episcopal church documents indicate work on the Nenana mission began in approximately 1907 across the river from the Native village. Its location was ostensibly to minimize any negative influences associated with the village. (Episcopal Archdeacon Hudson Stuck later lamented that the influences of a railroad town next to the mission were even worse.)

Over several years a church, school building, dormitory, small hospital and other facilities were completed. The boarding school, which could house about 40 students, attracted children from all over the Interior and in time a second village formed adjacent to the mission.

Events such as the arrival of the railroad and the 1920 influenza epidemic changed the nature of Nenana and led to a gradual decline in the Native population. The boarding school was forced to close in 1955.

The original mission site has been lost to river erosion. The current St. Mark's Church vicar, Marilyn Duggar, told me it was a tearful day when the last mission building fell into the encroaching Tanana River. Her mother had been a nurse at the mission, and they both stood forlornly on the bank as the structure floated past.

One of the few reminders of this earlier period is St. Mark's Church (shown in the drawing) in downtown Nenana. It was moved about a mile downriver from the mission's original site in 1955 after the mission school was closed.

The picturesque church is similar in design to other Episcopal mission churches throughout Interior Alaska—a log structure with gable front and bell tower. The 22 foot by 28 foot building is constructed of logs squared on three sides, with the bottom courses of logs flaring outwards. Gothic arched windows contain stained glass, and the building is topped by a shake roof.

Its interior is just as charming, with a hand-carved altar, and altar covering adorned with Athabascan beadwork on bleached moosehide. Visitors are welcome to tour the church when services are not being held.

Sources:

- *Alaska Community Database*. Alaska Department of Community and Regional Affairs. 2012
- *Alaska Today*, no author cited, Episcopal Church Missions House. 1936
- Conversation with Marilyn Duggar, Vicar at St. Mark's Episcopal Church
- *Modern Foragers: Wild Resource Use in Nenana Village, Alaska, Technical Paper No. 91*. Anne Shinkwin & Martha Case. Alaska Dept. of Fish and Game. 1984
- Photos of Nenana Episcopal Mission, from Walter and Lillian Phillips Photograph Collection, University of Alaska Fairbanks, Archives
- *The Alaskan Missions of the Episcopal Church, a Brief Sketch, Historical and Descriptive*. Hudson Stuck. Domestic and Foreign Missionary Society. 1920

Parks Highway, Nenana

Taku Chief before its retirement in 1978

Taku Chief a relic of Civil Aeronautics Administration's riverboat days

When the tug boat Taku Chief began its career in Southeast Alaska in 1938, the age of steamboating on Interior Alaska rivers was dying. Gold mining, which had spurred a few decades of frenetic activity along the Yukon River and its tributaries, was waning. Airplanes were taking over much of the freight and passenger service, and diesel and gasoline engines were beginning to replace steam as boat propulsion systems.

By the 1920s only two large river navigation operations remained: the Alaska Railroad (based out of Nenana), which operated steamboats from Fairbanks on the Chena River down to Marshall on the Yukon River; and the American-Yukon Navigation Company (AYNC, a subsidiary of the White Pass and Yukon Railway), which controlled river navigation from Tanana upriver to Canada. Several smaller navigation companies survived by serving small communities beneath the notice of the two giants, and by plying the smaller tributaries of the Yukon River.

Interestingly, the rise of air travel also brought about the entry of another river navigation operation in Interior Alaska. The Civil Aeronautics Administration (CAA, a precursor to the Federal Aviation Administration) was tasked with helping to build and maintain the infrastructure required by Alaska's fledgling aviation industry. Beginning in 1939 the CAA began constructing and improving air fields and installing and operating radio communications facilities throughout Alaska. In order to ferry workers and supplies around Interior Alaska the CAA was pressed into the river navigation business, requisitioning several boats to serve its needs.

The CAA acquired the Taku Chief in 1945 and moved it to Interior Alaska. The boat has two diesel engines, is 59 feet long and has a beam of 18 feet. It only draws 30 inches of water, so it was ideal for navigating Interior rivers. In a biography of Edgar Nollner Sr., who was a river pilot for the CAA, Nollner says the Taku Chief worked on the Tanana, Yukon and Koyukuk rivers while he was with the CAA. He also states that it ran with a five-man crew: captain, pilot, two engineers and a cook.

The Taku Chief probably operated on other Interior rivers as well. Bureau of Land Management documents indicate CAA boats also used to run supplies up the Kantishna River as far as Lake Minchumina.

In 1956 the Taku Chief was acquired by Yutana Barge Lines, which had not even existed a few years previously. The Alaska Railroad's riverboat commerce had steadily declined for years due to inroads by air service and smaller, more efficient boats. The AYNC had already thrown in the towel, selling its Alaska operations to the Alaska Railroad in 1943. In 1950 the Alaska Railroad stopped all passenger boat service and in 1955 it ceased riverboat operations entirely.

Several of the smaller river navigation businesses saw an opportunity and formed a partnership to bid on the railroad's riverboat operations. At first called B&R Tug and Barge, the winning bidders soon became Yutana Barge Lines. Yutana, which was based in Nenana, carved out a successful niche for itself. Most freight and passengers still traveled to villages in Interior Alaska by plane, but large freight and bulk fuel deliveries still had to be delivered via boat and barge. Yutana had become virtually the only freight carrier on the Yukon River and its tributaries before being acquired by Crowley Maritime Corporation in 2005.

After 40 years of service, the Taku Chief was retired in 1978. It now rests in Nenana, on land between the Parks Highway and A Street, greeting people as they enter town.

Sources:

- "Air Transportation," chapter 4-12 of *Alaska's Heritage*. Alaska Humanities Forum website. 2004
- *Edgar Nollner, Sr., a Biography*. Dr. Wendy H. Arundale. Yukon Koyukuk School District. 1985
- Informational signs at Taku Chief tug boat in Nenana.
- *Mukluk Telegraph* (Civil Aeronautics Administration Alaska newsletter). July-August 1945
- "River Transportation," chapter 4-9 of *Alaska's Heritage*, Alaska Humanities Forum website, 2004
- *"Tanana River Navigability Report." Ralph Basner. U.S. Bureau of Land Management. 2002*
- *Yukon River Steamboats*. Stan Cohen. Pictorial Histories Publishing Company. 1982

Parks Highway, Ester

Ester Assay in 1989

Ester assay office, a little building that endured

Many people are familiar with the hotel and Malemute Saloon at Ester Gold Camp. But how many have paid any attention to the small frame-building on the northeast corner of the gold camp property? Most other buildings on the property were built after 1930, but this little cabin was probably constructed about 1906, soon after Ester was established.

Thousands of miners flooded into the Fairbanks area after the 1902 discovery of gold on Pedro Creek. Gold was found on Ester Creek in 1903 and the small community of Ester City sprang up in 1904. Within a few years Ester boasted three hotels, five saloons plus other businesses, and a population of several hundred people.

As with most small towns around Fairbanks, the richest diggings around Ester began to play out fairly quickly. Ester's population dwindled in tandem with gold production, but the little town hung on.

The National Register of Historic Places nomination form for Ester Camp Historic District indicates the Fairbanks Exploration Company (FE Company) began acquiring claims and doing exploratory drilling along Ester Creek in the mid-1920s in preparation for large-scale dredging.

The company moved its Dredge No. 6 from Goldstream to Ester Creek and began dredging in the early 1930s. It built a mess hall/bunkhouse and related buildings in 1933 to support its Ester operations, and also acquired existing buildings such as the one shown in the drawing (which was used as an assay office) and moved them to the new camp's location.

Dredges float in their own little ponds, and the dredges (plus their ponds) slowly move along as the gold-bearing gravel is excavated. John Boswell's history of the FE Company relates that Dredge No. 6 gradually moved in this manner from Ester to Eva Creek, and then floated to Gold Hill via a specially constructed canal. In the winter of 1959 a stripped-down Dredge No. 6 (still weighing 680 tons) was pulled overland to Sheep Creek by 18 tractors.

With the dredge relocating to Sheep Creek, the Ester facilities were no longer needed. The camp was sold in 1958 and the new owners turned the property into a resort. The bunkhouse/mess hall was converted to a hotel, and one of the other camp buildings (also believed to date back to 1906) was refurbished as the Malemute Saloon.

Ester Gold Camp is much the same as it was when the FE Company sold it. It was added to the National Register of Historic Places in 1987. The little building that served as the company assay office is still there.

There doesn't appear to be any record of what its use was before the FE Company acquired it, but it was undoubtedly moved to the site from another location. Matthew Reckard, an Ester resident and historian, told me the assay building did not appear on a site map of the area done in the fall of 1933 (Mineral Survey 1652). Other FE Company buildings do appear on that survey.

Since the camp passed into private ownership, the assay building has seen many different uses, including snack shop, ticket booth and gift shop. I think it's a lovely little frame building, typical of the early 1900s when construction materials were in short supply.

Sources:

- Correspondence with Matthew Reckard, Ester resident and historian
- "Ester Camp Historic District National Register of Historic Places Inventory-Nomination Form." Wendy Arundale. National Park Service. 1985
- "Ester Myth 'Berried.'" Matthew Reckard. *The Ester Republic.* Vol. 1, No. 1, January 1999
- *Historic Resources in the Fairbanks North Star Borough.* Janet Matheson & F. Bruce Haldeman. Fairbanks North Star Borough. 1981
- *History of Alaska Operations of Unites States Smelting, Refining and Mining Company.* John Boswell. Mineral Industries Research Laboratory, University of Alaska, Fairbanks. 1979
- "The Discovery of Gold on Ester Creek." Matthew Reckard. *The Ester Republic.* Vol. 1, No. 3, March 1999

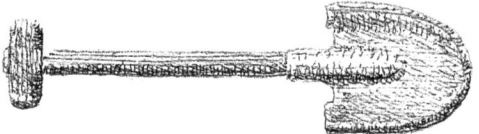

Parks Highway, Ester

Malemute Saloon in 1990

At the Malemute Saloon

A bunch of the boys were whooping it up in the Malamute Saloon;
The kid that handles the music-box was hitting a jag-time tune;
Back of the bar, in a solo game, sat Dangerous Dan McGrew,
And watching his luck was his light-o'-love, the lady that's known as Lou.

(from "The Shooting of Dan McGrew" by Robert Service)

This is a drawing of the Malemute Saloon, located at Ester Gold Camp in Ester. The gold camp was a support facility for gold dredges operated in the Ester area by the Fairbanks Exploration Company (FE Company). With the winding down of Ester area dredging in the late 1950s, the camp was sold to a group of private investors in 1958 and the new owners turned the property into a resort.

One of their first efforts was to open the Malemute Saloon. The saloon is within the Ester Camp Historic District, and according to the nomination form for the National Register of Historic Places, the building (believed to date back to about 1906 and probably moved from another location) was originally a garage before being converted into the saloon.

The owners added a false front to the metal-sided one-story building, and for more historical ambiance, acquired the bar counter from the Royal Alexandria Hotel in Dawson City. Half of the counter was installed in the saloon and the other half was stored next door (probably in the old blacksmith shop). This turned out to be a wise decision. When the Malemute Saloon burned down on June 3, 1969, the owners were able to rebuild, install the other half of the bar counter, and be back in business as good as ever.

The Malemute was well-known for its sawdust-covered floor, period décor, Robert Service poetry and lively entertainment. Contrary to popular myth, however, the saloon had no direct association with Robert Service or his poem, "The Shooting of Dan McGrew. " The closest association is the bar counter in the saloon, which, as I stated earlier, came from Dawson City.

Service also hailed from Dawson City for a time, but even then, "The Shooting of Dan McGrew" was written before Service ever set foot there. Service began working for the Bank of Canada in 1903, and his first posting in the Yukon Territory was at Whitehorse in 1904.

He was already a bit of a poet, and according the biography, *Robert Service – Under the Spell of the Yukon*, Stroller White, editor of the Whitehorse newspaper, urged Service to write poetry with a local flavor, to "give us something about our own little bit of earth."

It was in Whitehorse that Service first listened to the sourdoughs' yarns that gave him ideas for his poetry. "The Shooting of Dan McGrew' was written there in 1906 and first printed in Service's book, *Songs of a Sourdough*. The book was published in 1907, one year before Service moved to Dawson City.

Service lived in the Yukon off and on for about eight years — five of those as an employee of the Bank of Canada. As far as I can tell, there is no evidence that he ever visited Ester or Fairbanks.

Ester Gold Camp and the Malemute closed in 2010. The camp sat vacant for over 10 years until re-opening in 2021 under new ownership. The new owners, with experience restoring old buildings, are revitalizing Ester Gold Camp; and the Malemute is now back in business.

Sources:

- "Ester Camp Historic District National Register of Historic Places Inventory-Nomination Form." Wendy Arundale. National Park Service. 1986
- "Ester venue combines history and entertainment."
- Alena Naiden. In *Fairbanks Daily News-Miner*. 5-23-
- 2021
- *History of Alaska Operations of Unites States Smelting, Refining and Mining Company*. John Boswell. Mineral Industries Research Laboratory, University of Alaska, Fairbanks. 1979
- *Historic Resources in the Fairbanks North Star Borough*. Janet Matheson & F. Bruce Haldeman. Fairbanks North Star Borough. 1981
- *Robert Service – Under the Spell of the Yukon*. Enid Mallory. Heritage House Publishing. 2006
- "The Truth about the Ester Gold Camp Buildings." Matthew Reckard. In *The Ester Republic*. May-June 2002

Elliott Highway, Manley

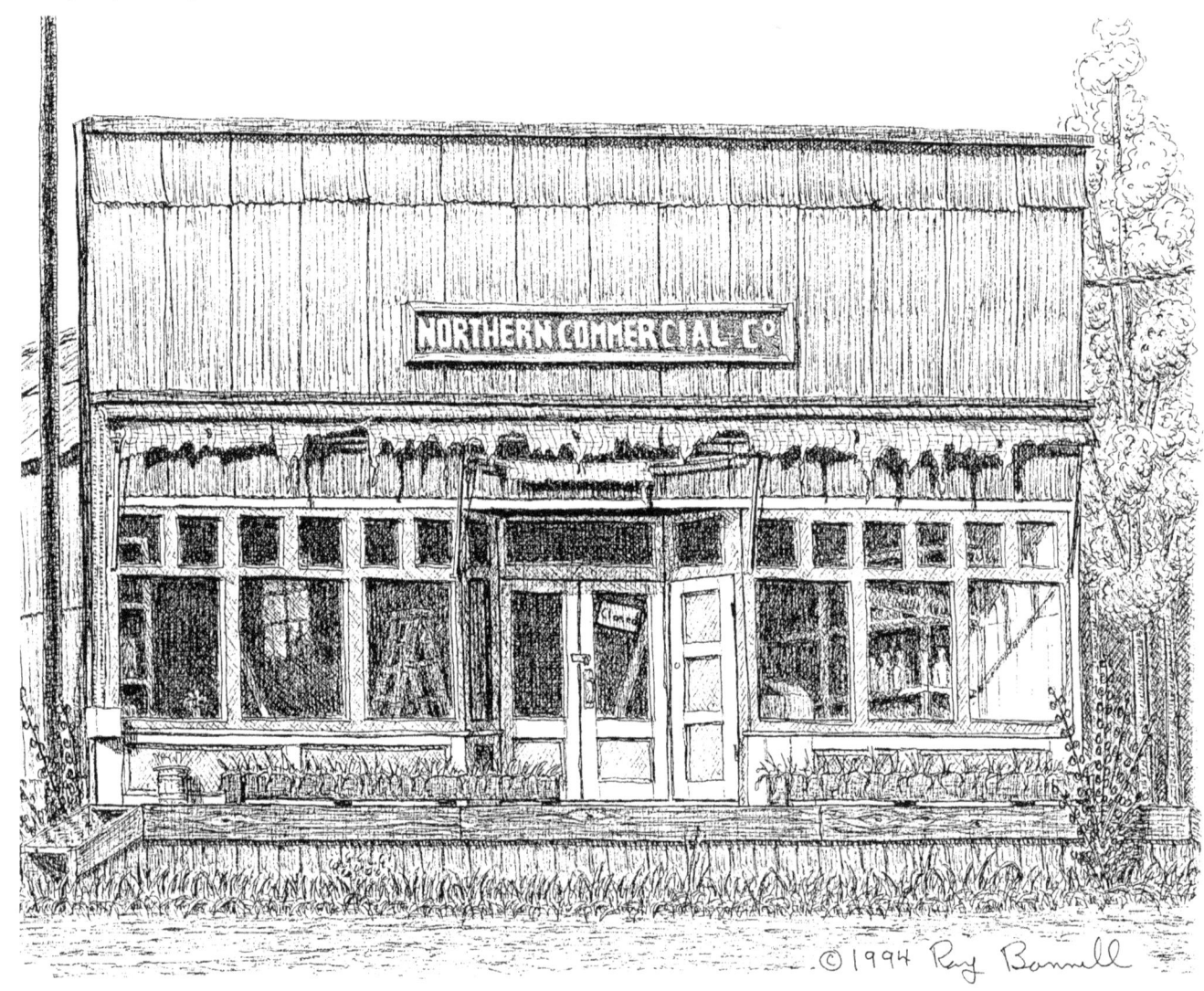

Manley NC Company store in 1993

Manley's Northern Commercial Company store filled with memories

Manley Hot Springs (usually just called Manley) is located west of Fairbanks, about 75 miles as the raven flies. But if you want to travel there by car you drive north to Fox, northwest to Livengood, and then southwest to Manley Hot Springs, a total of about 160 miles. Most of the way you travel through the White Mountains via the Elliott Highway (named for Malcolm Elliott, president of the Alaska Road Commission from 1927 to 1932).

The town is at the end of the road. (Well almost the end of the road. Manley sits on the banks of a Tanana River slough, and the highway continues three miles to Tanana River Landing.) Manley is a small village of about 100 people, but a century ago it boasted 500 residents.

According to a University of Alaska report on geothermal activity at Manley Hot Springs, the community was established in 1902 when a prospector named John Karshner discovered the hot springs and started a homestead. The United States Army built a telegraph station at nearby Baker Creek as part of the Washington-Alaska Military Cable and Telegraph System (WAMCATS) at about the same time.

The community was called Baker Hot Springs (after the nearby creek) but quickly became know just as "Hot Springs." It soon became a supply and community center for miners from the nearby Eureka and Tofty areas to the north. Eventually a telegraph station was established there. By 1906 Karshner had built-up a large operation with hog, poultry and dairy barns, greenhouses, and truck garden—all heated from the hot springs. His and other farms in the area produced fresh meat and produce for the hungry miners.

Frank Manley built the Hot Springs Resort Hotel in 1907. (The town was officially renamed Manley Hot Springs in 1957.) His resort attracted visitors from all over Interior Alaska. Guests could be dropped off by riverboat at the Tanana River landing, or they could take the two-day overland stage from Fairbanks.

The town prospered by supplying the mines and catering to the hot springs guests, and the Alaska Commercial Company decided to open a store there. Lois Kitchener's book, *Flag over the North, the Story of the Northern Commercial Company*, tells of Alaska Commercial owning a string of trading posts and stores across Alaska, as well as a navigation and transportation operation. It became the Northern Commercial Company (NC Company) in 1922, and sold groceries and general merchandise in its stores.

In many small settlements, the NC Company store also acted as the post office, social center and bank. It was no different in Manley, especially after the resort burned to the ground in 1913. As with many of the smaller towns in Interior Alaska, the area's population withered after the Gold Rush, declining to about 30 residents by 1920.

The NC Company store in Manley remained open until the mid 1960s when declining population forced it to close. The drawing shows the store front in 1994, when there were still goods sitting on some of the store's shelves.

Today the town has one seasonal hotel (the Manley Roadhouse), a laundromat with showers, gas station, school, post office, museum and grocery store. The hot springs still flow, and I understand that a couple of local residents run a greenhouse with water from the springs. For the right price you can soak in hot tubs inside the greenhouse surrounded by exotic (for Alaska) foliage. It would be a nice way to end a day in a small Alaska village filled with memories and friendly people.

Sources:

- *Alaska Community Database*. Alaska Department of Community and Regional Affairs. 2011
- *Dictionary of Alaska Place Names, Geological Survey professional paper 567*. Donald J. Orth. U.S. Geological Survey. 1971
- *Flag over the North, the Story of the Northern Commercial Company*. Lois Delano Kitchener. Superior Publishing Company. 1954
- *Manley Hot Springs*. Rainer J. Newberry & Diana N. Solie. Department of Geology & Geophysics, University of Alaska, Fairbanks. 2011

Elliott Highway, Livengood

Livengood garage in 2000

Mining camps merge to form Livengood in 1915

In the spring of 1914, two Ester miners, Jay Livengood and Nathaniel "Teddy" Hudson, tramped off to the headwaters of the Tolovana River (about 60 miles northwest of Fairbanks) to prospect for richer diggings. The area had been scouted numerous times already, but color was about all that had been found.

Livengood and Hudson found promising paystreaks and staked claims on Livengood, Gertrude and Olive Creeks during July and August. They returned to Ester for supplies and then scurried back to the Tolovana with their partners: Michael Beegler, J. C. Kinney, Gus Conradt, George Wheeler and Teddy's brothers, James and Clifford.

Although this little expedition was supposedly secret, word leaked out and a small stampede headed to the Tolovana. Audrey Parker's book, *Livengood, the Last Stampede*, describes four camps that sprang up in the area. Lake City developed three miles below Discovery claim on Livengood Creek (probably near where the Elliott Highway now crosses the creek). Livengood City spread around the creek's Discovery claim, and Brooks City was just upstream. In addition, Olive City was located on Olive Creek, about two miles to the east.

Olive City and Lake City quickly disappeared when richer diggings were located elsewhere. By the end of 1915, Brooks City (which had merged with Livengood City) was the surviving camp.

The town's name was shortened to Brooks, but it did not retain that name for long. When residents applied for a post office that same year, postal officials feared that mail bound for Brooks, Alaska, would be confused with mail headed for Brooks, Alabama. Consequently, the town's name changed back to Livengood.

As with many of Interior Alaska's mining areas, underground drifting was the principal mining method. Eventually, as in Fairbanks, dredging was introduced. In the late 1930s, Livengood Placers Inc. brought in a dredge similar to ones used by the Fairbanks Exploration Company. Unfortunately, the venture was unprofitable and dredging ceased before World War II. The dredge was eventually moved to the Koyukuk River area. Mining has continued off and on over the years, and by 1990, more than 460,000 ounces of gold had been recovered from Livengood mines.

When Livengood was established, access was via the winding Tolovana River, or a 60-mile trail from Fairbanks. Residents quickly clamored for better access, and by the fall of 1915 the Alaska Road Commission had blazed a rough wagon road from Olnes, a stop on the Tanana Valley Railroad just north of Fairbanks. The wagon road was upgraded in the 1930s and eventually extended to Manley Hot Springs in the 1950s. This road is now the Elliott Highway.

The state of Alaska improved the Elliott Highway in the 1970s. Livengood was bypassed in the process and is now about two miles off the highway. The old highway used to wind along the ridges above Livengood Creek before dropping down into town. The cabins in the drawing are at the bottom of the old road coming off the ridge. A friend of mine, whose uncle lived and mined at Livengood, says these cabins used to house the town garage. The upper log cabin was the office, and the lower frame structure was where vehicles were worked on.

Most of the town's buildings have been destroyed or have fallen into ruins, but there are still enough left to evoke memories of its pioneer days. Please respect private property if you visit.

Sources:

- Conversations with Jim Deininger, retired BLM geologist (his uncle mines at Livengood). 2012
- *Dictionary of Alaska Place Names, Geological Survey professional paper 567.* Donald J. Orth. U.S. Geological Survey. 1971
- *Livengood, the Last Stampede.* Audrey Parker. Hats off Books. 2004
- *The Northern Gold Fleet, Twentieth Century Gold Dredging in Alaska.* Clark C. Spence. University of Illinois Press. 1996

Elliott Highway, Olnes

Olnes outhouse in 1990

Olnes outhouse has distinctive character

Olnes is pretty much just a spot on the map these days. It is about 20 miles north of Fairbanks along the Elliott Highway. A sign there (dating back to at least 1990) says "Entering Olnes City, Pop. 1." While there are several subdivisions in the surrounding hills, only a handful of people live in the immediate area, but it used to be a thriving little community.

The town, named after Nels Olnes, a Norwegian prospector, was a regular stop on the Tanana Valley Railroad between 1907 and 1930. The railroad had a depot there, as well as warehouse and machine shop. Olnes, with a population of 300 people, also boasted a general store, hotel, several saloons, boarding house, post office and livery stable, as well as numerous cabins and houses.

Olnes is located on the north side of the hills that separate Fairbanks from the Chatanika River valley. According to the book, *Tanana Valley Railroad, the Gold Dust Line,* locomotives needed a full head of steam to make it over the hills, and Olnes was the only dependable source of water between the station at Chatanika (the end of the line at mile 39.2) and the one at Gilmore (on the Fairbanks side of the hills at mile 20).

There was a small creek several hundred yards east of Olnes proper and the railroad erected a water tank there where locomotives could take on water before heading up the grade.

The small hamlet was also a trans-shipment point for the mining areas near Livengood and Tolovana about 50 miles to the north. Trains ferried passengers and freight from Fairbanks to Olnes, and horse-drawn wagons provided transport from Olnes out to the isolated mining camps. In return, those same wagons brought gold dust back to Olnes for shipment on the trains to Fairbanks.

As with many smaller mining communities around Fairbanks, Olnes dwindled away after the easy gold had been recovered. And when the railroad shut down in 1930 Olnes fate was sealed. It did not suffer the ignominious demise of places such as Chatanika and Eldorado City, however, where entire towns quickly disappeared as buildings were destroyed or moved to make way for gold dredges.

At Olnes, the town just faded away. Its buildings slowly collapsed, or were moved or torn apart to recycle the construction materials. Almost all of the town's original buildings are gone. There used to be a small false-front building adjacent to the Elliott Highway that operated as a store up until the 1970s, but it burned down in the early 1990s.

There are still several buildings there, but according to borough land office records, most of them were built after the town's heyday. The only structure left that might date from the early 1900s is a small outhouse located along the old railroad right-of-way. I have talked with friends who grew up in the area and remember using the outhouse.

The picturesque outhouse has a wood-shake roof with decorative ridge-line, iron filigree decoration at the gables, and a diamond shaped window. The interior was decorated with red brocade wall paper — the same type of wall paper I found in an old cabin near Old Chatanika, six miles away.

It would seem, from the care lavished on the building, that someone spent a lot of time in this outhouse. It is located on private property.

Sources:

- Conversations with Elizabeth Cook and Steve Hormann, who used to live in the area.
- Fairbanks North Star Borough property records
- *Historic Resources in the Fairbanks North Star Borough*. Janet Matheson & F. Bruce Haldeman. Fairbanks North Star Borough. 1981
- *Tanana Valley Railroad, the Gold Dust Line*. Nicholas Deely. Denali Designs. 1996

Steese Highway, Fox

Gold Dredge No. 8 in 1992

Gold Dredge No. 8, a giant that helped save Fairbanks

The Fairbanks Exploration Company's Gold Dredge No. 8 at Fox (shown in the drawing) is perhaps the most visible and well-known dredge in the Fairbanks area, but the FE Company actually operated eight of these giants near town. No. 3 can be seen at Chatanika.

Five others are tucked away from sight: No. 2 on Fairbanks Creek, No. 3 at Chatanika, No. 5 at Dome Creek, No. 6 on Sheep Creek and No. 10 at Cripple Creek. Dredge No. 4 (operated on Pedro Creek) was dismantled in 1959 and moved to Chicken, and No. 7 (at Fish Creek) was demolished when Fort Knox gold mine was developed.

The Fairbanks dredges were not the first ones in the North. According to the book, *The Northern Gold Fleet: Twentieth-Century Gold Dredging in Alaska,* dredges were operating in the Canadian Klondike by 1900 — eventually about two dozen worked there. On the far western side of Alaska, ancient tundra-covered beaches containing rich gold deposits were discovered in the Nome area in 1905, and by the mid-1910s there were at least a dozen dredges in that area. All told, there were about 50 dredges scattered across the territory before World War II.

These gold dredges were immense structures, and their use predicated the availability of relatively inexpensive and reliable means of freighting heavy equipment into the country. The Klondike dredges came by ocean to Skagway, were shipped via the White Pass and Yukon Railroad to Whitehorse, and then transferred to steamboats for the final leg to Dawson City. Dredges on the Seward Peninsula were shipped the entire way via ocean-going vessels. A few small wooden-hulled dredges were brought into Fairbanks by steamboats in the 1910s, but with the opening of the Alaska Railroad in 1923 large gold dredges finally arrived in the area.

Dredges are essentially floating gold processing plants. Most in Alaska were "bucket-line" dredges that used a continuous line of heavy steel buckets (the digging ladder) to scoop gold-bearing gravel from the bottom of a man-made pond.

The gravel was dumped onto screens and washed — the heavy gold being separated and the waste rock (tailings) dumped into tailing piles out the back of the dredge. These dredges could economically work ground with extremely low gold concentrations and recovered about 96 percent. The Oakland Museum of California (gold dredging was a huge industry in California) reports that on average it took 250 giant dredge buckets filled with gravel to produce one ounce of gold!

Constructed in 1928, Gold Dredge No. 8 is five-stories tall and weighs 1,065 tons. The bow gantry is 43 feet tall and supports a belt-driven bucket line containing 68 steel buckets. Each bucket holds six cubic-feet and weighs 1,583 pounds. The bucket line could tear gravel from 35 feet below water level.

As impressive as that sounds, No. 8 was one of the smaller dredges in the FE Company's fleet. The largest dredges in Fairbanks sported 10 cubic-foot buckets and could reach down 60 feet. Some dredges outside Alaska had 18 cubic-foot buckets and could reach gravel 170 feet below water level.

No. 8 was shut down permanently in 1959. During its 30 years of operation it traveled 4.5 miles and recovered 7.5 million ounces of gold.

In 1982, John and Ramona Reeves bought Gold Dredge No. 8 and the land on which it sits. They then acquired the bunkhouse from the FE Company's Goldstream Camp and moved it to a spot adjacent to the dredge. The next year they opened the site for public tours. The Reeves later bought much of the other FE Company property around Fairbanks and moved equipment and buildings from other locations to the dredge's site.

Gold Dredge No. 8 was listed as a National Historic Site in 1984 and as a National Historical Mechanical Engineering Landmark in 1986. The Binkley family (which operates the Riverboat Discovery) now owns the dredge, and after several years of closure, it is once again open to the public.

Sources:

- *Alaska Gold: The History of Gold Dredge No. 8*. Maria Reeves. Gold Fever Press. 2009
- "Giant Gold Machines - Gold Dredges," in *Gold Fever*. Oakland Museum of California website, 2008
- "Gold Dredge No. 8 National Register of Historic Places Inventory-Nomination Form." John Reeves. National Park Service. 1983
- *History of Alaska Operations of Unites States Smelting, Refining and Mining Company*. John Boswell. Mineral Industries Research Laboratory, University of Alaska, Fairbanks. 1979
- *The Northern Gold Fleet: Twentieth-Century Gold Dredging in Alaska*. Clark C. Spence. University of Illinois Press. 1996

Steese Highway, Fairbanks Creek

Fairbanks Creek: mining camps, churn drills and gold dredges

Churn Drill on Fairbanks Creek tailings in 1995

When I visited Fairbanks Creek in the 1990s there were several old churn drills sitting on the dredge tailings, obscured by trees. They had probably been sitting there for 30 years. (Look closely at the tree in front of the drill.) These drills, used to obtain ore samples, were essential for successful gold dredging. Dredges in Fairbanks operated on a slim profit margin — made even slimmer since the gold-bearing gravels were covered by varying thicknesses of overburden (silt and frozen "muck") that had to be stripped away.

In his book about the Fairbanks Exploration Company (FE Company), John Boswell (the company's retired manager) wrote that as rule of thumb, any ground that had been good enough for drifting (underground mining of placer gold deposits) could be dredged profitably. However, that did not mean the dredges could indiscriminately plow up the land. The dredges followed predetermined paths based on drilling results. Systematic drilling provided data to estimate the amount of overburden to be stripped, the volume of gravel to be dredged, and the amount of gold that could be recovered. One of the deepest holes drilled on Fairbanks Creek showed 152 feet of overburden and 144 feet of gravel.

Fairbanks Creek, 20 miles northeast of Fairbanks and just east of Cleary Summit, was the site for two separate dredging operations. It also had more gold camps than most creeks in the Fairbanks area. Ester and Cleary Creeks each had two camps, but Fairbanks Creek boasted three.

The earliest camp was Meehan, which grew near the claims of three brothers: Matt, Pat and Tom Meehan. Communities also sprang up at Alder Creek Camp (one mile to the east) and at Fairbanks Creek Camp (three miles to the southeast). In reality, mines, cabins and businesses were located all along the creek, and in the 1910s there may have been about 1500 people living along the creek.

It may be that the different camp names just represent different times periods. According to the Fairbanks North Star Borough Planning Department, Meehan began around 1905 and mining activity there petered out in the early 1930s. Next came Alder Creek Camp, established in 1939. Finally, Fairbanks Creek Camp came into being in 1949.

During the "Meehan period" and about the time drift mining played out in the late 1910s, activity on the creek was re-invigorated when one of the earliest dredging operations in the Fairbanks area began. The Fairbanks Gold Dredge Company (FGDC), also called the "English Company" since it was English-owned, subleased some of the Meehan brothers' claims. It built a support camp (add one more camp to the list), moved in a small dredge, and in 1919 began dredging.

The FGDC's first dredge originally operated on the Stewart River above Dawson City in Canada, but was disassembled and shipped via The Yukon and Tanana Rivers to Chena, near the confluence of the Chena and Tanana Rivers. Then it was transferred to the Tanana Valley Railroad and shipped to Gilmore, a few miles northeast of Fox. From there it was freighted overland by wagon and reassembled.

The company also built and operated a second dredge on Fish Creek (the present location of the Fort Knox mine). A third dredge was constructed in 1928 to replace the first one which had worn out. The FGDC dredges ran until 1931 when the company went into receivership.

The FE Company bought the FGDC assets and in 1949 moved its gold dredge No. 2 from Goldstream Creek to Fairbanks Creek. The company also built Fairbanks Creek Camp to support the dredge operations. Dredge No. 2 operated until 1963, which was the year the FE Company permanently closed down its remaining dredges. The old dredge still sits in its dredge pond at the lower end of the creek, with the remains of Fairbanks Creek Camp about a mile away.

Sources:

- *Dictionary of Alaska Place Names*. Donald Orth. U.S. Geological Survey. 1971
- "Gold Placers of the Fairbanks District, Alaska." L. M. Prindle. *Contributions to Economic Geology, bulletin No. 225*. U.S. Geological Survey. 1904
- *History of Alaskan Operations of United States Smelting, Refining and Mining Company*. John C. Boswell. Mineral Industry Research Laboratory, University of Alaska, Fairbanks. 1979
- "Mining in the Fairbanks District." Theodore Chapin, *Mineral Resources of Alaska. Bulletin No. 692*. U.S. Geological Survey. 1917
- *The Northern Gold Fleet: Twentieth-Century Gold Dredging in Alaska*. Clark C. Spence. University of Illinois Press. 1996

Steese Highway, Fairbanks Creek

Eagan cabin at Meehan in 1995

Meandering mining camp? Where is Meehan?

Where, oh, where, oh, where is Meehan? That's what you might wonder looking at different U.S. Geological Survey maps of Fairbanks Creek. Meehan, active during the early 1900s, was a mining community about 20 miles northeast of Fairbanks. Early maps show it upstream from the confluence of Alder and Fairbanks Creeks, but later maps show it about a mile or so downstream.

In a 1968 article in *Alaska Sportsman Magazine* titled "The Silent Creek," Isabel Eagan Richards (who grew up at Meehan) writes that the town was on the north bank of

Fairbanks Creek at Discovery claim (the first mining claim staked on a creek). That would place the town where older maps show it—west of Alder Creek.

Later maps may be in error because Alder Creek moved. The *Dictionary of Alaska Place Names* indicates that Alder Creek's channel was altered by mining, and its outlet at Fairbanks Creek moved about one-half mile to the west. It may be that some mapmaker, confused by the surveyor's notes, moved the town to the east rather than move the creek to the west.

The town was established in about 1905, after the Meehan brothers (Matt, Pat and Tom) staked the Discovery claim (and most other claims along Fairbanks Creek.) The town was the center of social life on Fairbanks Creek during the early 1900s and had a post office, several stores and roadhouses, two dance halls, a restaurant, four saloons and a school. In 1907 it had 300 residents, with maybe another thousand living in the surrounding area.

Isabel Richards' father, Dan Eagan Sr., walked the 380-mile Valdez-Fairbanks Trail in 1908 and ended up working as a bookkeeper for a Meehan merchant. By 1913 Dan was doing well enough that he and his partner, George Griffin, bought the store, renaming it Eagan and Griffin General Merchandise. That same year, Dan brought his childhood sweetheart, Isabelle, to Alaska, married her, and they set up housekeeping on Fairbanks Creek. The Eagans raised seven children there.

Eagan and Griffin General Merchandise sold a little bit of everything and was a social center for the area. (It was also the post office.) At the center of its large main room was a big barrel stove surrounded by chairs.

The store also acted as agent for the two banks in Fairbanks: Washington-Alaska Bank and First National Bank. At the back of the store was a small room with a barred window, a counter with a large gold scale and large safe. It was there that miners brought their gold dust to be weighed and traded for currency. Isabel estimated that her father weighed out over $10 million in gold dust at the store.

By the 1930s, mining activities at Meehan had ebbed. In 1937 there were only a handful of residents, and in 1942 the post office closed. The store closed and was torn down, and the Eagan clan moved into Fairbanks, leaving the empty family home to decay.

Today all that remains at Meehan is part of Dan and Isabelle Eagan's home. Their home, which stood next to the store, originally was a large two-story log and frame house. The main part of the home has collapsed and disappeared, and all that remains is what used to be the family kitchen.

Sources:

Conversations with Pete Eagan, John Cook and Virginia Shafer (grandchildren of Dan and Isabelle Eagan)
Dictionary of Alaska Place Names, Geological Survey professional paper 567. Donald J. Orth. U.S. Geological Survey. 1971
Directory of Alaska Post Offices and Postmasters 1896-1964. Melvin Ricks. Tongass Publishing Company. 1965
"Forgotten Freighter of Fairbanks Creek," in *Heartland Magazine.* Joe Ashley. *Fairbanks Daily News-Miner.* October 8, 1989
Historic Resources in the Fairbanks North Star Borough, by Janet Matheson & Bruce Haldeman, 1981
"The Silent Creek." Isabel Eagan Richards. *Alaska Sportsman Magazine*. 3-part series in July, August and September issues, 1968

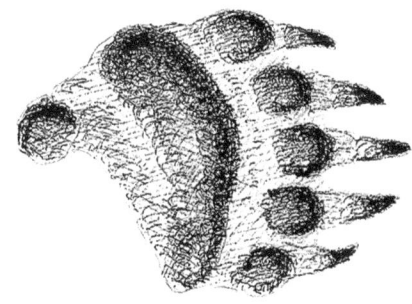

Steese Highway, Little Eldorado Creek

Eldorado Station in 1993

All that's left of Eldorado

The Tanana Valley Railroad (which operated from 1905 to 1930 under various names and owners) used to run 35 miles from Fairbanks to Chatanika through country that, although close to town, probably relatively few people have seen. The TVRR followed the route of the present-day Alaska Railroad right-of-way from Fairbanks to the Goldstream Valley, then along Goldstream to Fox and the old townsite of Gilmore, and over the hills to the old Olnes townsite about 20 miles north of Fairbanks (the Elliot Highway follows roughly the same route). Then the railroad right-of-way turned east-northeast and ran an additional six miles to Chatanika.

About half way from Olnes to Chatanika the railroad crossed Little Eldorado Creek, which flowed down from the Cleary Summit area to the south. Three miles up that creek was the bustling little mining hamlet of Eldorado

City, so it was natural that a small train station was established at Little Eldorado Creek and a road constructed to Eldorado City. For many years the building in this drawing was identified as "the" Eldorado Station.

However, according to Nicholas Deely's book, *Tanana Valley Railroad, the Gold Dust Line*, some old-timers say it is actually an Eldorado City building that was put on skids and hauled down the creek at a later date. Eldorado City is now gone. In fact, the town didn't even survive into the mid 1900s. The easy gold diggings in the Fairbanks area were exhausted by the mid 1910s, and many of the smaller gold camps such as Eldorado City just withered away. Even Fairbanks experienced a drastic population decrease.

Then the Fairbanks Exploration Company (FE Company) moved into the area in the 1920s, bought up mining claims along all the major creeks and began dredging. John Boswell's history of the FE Company relates that Eldorado City's buildings had to be moved or destroyed to make way for the dredge which began operations in 1947. So in either case, this is all that's left of Eldorado.

The old TVRR right-of-way through the Chatanika Valley passes through a lot of low-lying muskeg and marshy areas, and the building in the picture is pretty much impossible to get to except during winter. Back in the mid-1990s a group of us railroad buffs tried to walk the old right-of way from Olnes to Chatanika one summer, but when the ground under our feet started acting like Jello we turned back.

The ground along parts of the old right-of-way was unstable because the railroad's builders did nothing to prevent thawing of permafrost underlying the tracks. As the permafrost melted, they simply dumped more ballast (the gravel underneath the railroad ties) to buoy up the roadbed. Now during summer months the remaining roadbed in low-lying areas floats on top of the thawed saturated soils.

I was able to get out to Little Eldorado Creek by waiting until early October, after the ground had frozen but before deep snow covered the trail. Then I hiked in the three or so miles from the Chatanika end.

If you look closely at the drawing you will see a large post propped against the back of the building. There were actually about 10 or so posts back there holding the building up, and numerous small posts inside holding up the second floor. I haven't been out there in over 10 years, so who knows what is left of Eldorado now.

Sources:

- Fairbanks North Star Borough property records
- *Historic Resources in the Fairbanks North Star Borough*. Janet Matheson & F. Bruce Haldeman,.Fairbanks North Star Borough. 1981
- *Tanana Valley Railroad, the Gold Dust Line*,.Nicholas Deely. Denali Designs. 1996
- *History of Alaska Operations of United States Smelting, Refining and Mining Company*. John Boswell. Mineral Industries Research Laboratory, University of Alaska. 1979

Steese Highway, Chatanika

Seppala cabin in 1995

Leonhard Seppala's Chatanika cabin, a link to one of dog mushing's greats

Most people probably aren't aware that Leonhard (Sepp) Seppala, who achieved fame during the 1925 diphtheria serum run to Nome and popularized the use of Siberian huskies in sled dog racing, lived at Chatanika, Alaska for almost 20 years. (His cabin is shown in the drawing.)

Sepp emigrated from Norway to Alaska in 1900 and began working for the Pioneer Mining Company (PMC) at Nome. It was at a PMC mess hall that Sepp met his future wife, Constance. (She was a waitress there and he was the camp's mining foreman.) Eventually, Sepp become superintendent of the ditches vital for bringing water to the diggings.

He was introduced to dog mushing when his employer grubstaked three other men and him to a winter prospecting trip in the Kougarok area north of Nome. They traveled by dogsled, and although the prospecting trip came to naught, Sepp fell in love with mushing.

It was probably inevitable that men began racing their sled dogs (especially when they could bet on the outcome), and one of the first recorded long-distance races started in Nome. The All-Alaska Sweepstakes was a 408-mile race from Nome (on the south side of the Seward Peninsula) to Candle (on the north side) and back.

It was held annually from 1908 until 1917, when World War I emptied the area of military-aged young men and forced the race's demise. Sepp won the All-Alaska Sweepstakes three years straight— from 1915 to 1917. The first year he won, Constance was also crowned All-Alaska Sweepstakes queen.

PMC sold its operations to Hammon Consolidated Gold Fields Company in the 1920s, but Sepp continued working on the ditches. Hammon was eventually absorbed by U.S. Smelting, Mining and Refining Company (parent company of Fairbanks Exploration Company). When the FE Company began its Chatanika operations (about 30 road miles north of Fairbanks), Sepp transferred. According to a March 1929 issue of the *Fairbanks Daily-News-Miner* he became superintendent of the Davidson Ditch that year.

For his first few years in the Fairbanks area, Sepp worked on the Davidson Ditch in summer and raced his Siberian huskies in the Eastern U.S. and Canada during winter.

About 1930 he quit racing in the Lower 48 and returned to Alaska as a year-round resident. One of his few forays into racing outside Alaska after that was the 1932 Winter Olympics at Lake Placid in New York. Sled dog racing was a demonstration event that year and Sepp took a silver medal.

He also stayed active mushing in the Fairbanks area, participating in local races and winter festivals. The Seppalas' daughter, Sigrid, was crowned Miss Fairbanks during the 1937 winter festival.

When the Seppalas first moved to Fairbanks they lived in FE Company housing (the upstairs apartment a the Noyes House on Illinois Street).

According to *Historic Resources in the Fairbanks North Star Borough*, in the early 1930s the Seppalas built a small 16-foot by 16-foot log cabin just east of the newly established FE Company camp at Chatanika. They expanded the cabin over time. Photos from the 1940s show the cabin with a shed addition to the rear, along with a white picket fence and a huge flower garden. Later another small cabin was tacked onto the addition's east end.

The Steese Highway used to run right by the Seppalas' cabin, but was relocated to the base of the hill in later years. The road that runs in front of the cabin is now called Old Chatanika Road.

Sepp retired from the FE Company in 1946 and moved to Seattle, where he died in 1967. The book, *Seppala's Saga of the Sled Dog*, says Sepp once estimated that he had driven with his sled dogs more than a quarter of a million miles.

Sources:

- *"Historic resources of the Minnie Street corridor: final report."* Terrence Cole. Alaska DOT. 1989
- *History of Alaska Operations of Unites States Smelting, Refining and Mining Company.* John Boswell. Mineral Industries Research Laboratory, University of Alaska, Fairbanks. 1979
- "Reindeer, Gold and Scandal," in *Norwegian-American Studies, Volume 30.* Kenneth O. Byork. Norwegian-American Historical Association. 1985
- *Seppala's Saga of the Sled Dog, Volume 1 & 2.* Raymond Thompson. No publisher listed. 1970
- *Seppala, Alaska Dog Driver.* Elizabeth M. Ricker. Little, Brown & Company. 1930
- The Seppala collection. University of Alaska Fairbanks, Archives

Steese Highway, Chatanika

Chatanika schoolhouse in 1994

Chatanika schoolhouse, a historic preservation success story

If you enjoy tramping through the hills or along back roads looking for hidden gems—those out-of-the-way or forgotten buildings with lots of character—check out the old Chatanika schoolhouse near mile 28 of the Steese Highway.

The building sits on the hillside a half mile above Chatanika Gold Camp, an old Fairbanks Exploration Company operations camp. It is a modest one-story wood-frame structure, about 18 by 24-feet, surrounded by trees and commanding a lovely view of the Chatanika valley.

The schoolhouse actually started life at "Old" Chatanika, about three miles to the west. Old Chatanika (it began as just Chatanika) was established in about 1904. At its peak, the town was home to about 500 people. In 1912 the territory granted Chatanika permission to form its own school district, and the schoolhouse itself dates from the mid to late 1910s.

A photograph in the collection of the Circle District Historical Society shows the schoolhouse at Old Chatanika sometime between 1922-24, looking much the same as it does today. The caption on the photo notes that some of the pupils who lived at Eldorado City a few miles away came to school in a dog-powered cart along the Tanana Valley Railroad's tracks.

After the area's drift mines had exhausted the richest placer deposits, large dredges were brought in to process the lower grade gravels. According to John Boswell's history of the Fairbanks Exploration Company, the FE Company started dredging Lower Cleary Creek in 1928, and added another dredge on Upper Cleary Creek in 1929.

Before the dredges began churning up the ground, the company built a camp in 1924-25 to serve its Cleary Creek operations. The camp was located just about equidistant from Chatanika and another town called Cleary (two miles southeast). The community that grew around the camp quickly became known as "New" Chatanika, and residents from Cleary and Old Chatanika gravitated there. The FE Company acquired rights to claims all along Cleary Creek, including the land under Cleary and Old Chatanika, so it was inevitable that those two towns would disappear. Consequently, the school at Old Chatanika also relocated to New Chatanika, probably in the late-1920s. Along with the school came the schoolhouse (on skids).

The little school above New Chatanika taught students from all three communities and also served as a community hall. Its doors closed for lack of students in 1934, but re-opened briefly for the 1941-42 school year. (A federal government edict halting all gold production in the US for the duration of World War II probably had something to do with the final closure.)

After that the schoolhouse passed into private ownership and it's hard to say what the building was used for. When I visited in 1994, the structure was abandoned and askew. Windows were broken out, doors were missing, the floor and ceiling had gaping holes — it seemed destined for destruction.

However, in 2001 the schoolhouse and the land it sits on were acquired by Marlene Bach, a long-time resident of Chatanika (her father ran the trading post there for years). She has restored the schoolhouse and turned it into a museum filled with old photographs and exhibits, and the school's original desks and piano. The museum is closed during the winter, but in the summer I encourage you to go out and see it. The visit is well-worth the time.

Sources:

- "Cleary; a legend carved on the hillside," in *Heartland Magazine*. Fred Pratt. *Fairbanks Daily News-Miner* July 23, 1989
- Conversation with Marlene Bach, current owner of the schoolhouse
- *Dictionary of Alaska Place Names, Geological Survey professional paper 567.* Donald J. Orth. U.S. Geological Survey. 1971
- *History of Alaskan Operations of United States Smelting, Refining and Mining Company*, John C. Boswell. Mineral Industry Research Laboratory, University of Alaska, Fairbanks. 1979
- Photo of Chatanika Schoolhouse in 1920s, from Beistline photo collection. Circle District Historical Society
- *Tanana Valley Railroad, the Gold Dust Line*. Nicholas Deely. Denali Designs. 1996

Steese Highway, U.S. Creek

Ambitious Davidson Ditch brought water to Fairbanks dredges

U.S. Creek siphon in 2011

"Ditch" is such a mundane word and certainly doesn't accurately describe the Davidson Ditch, the 90-mile long system of open earthwork canals, steel pipe and tunnel that carried water from the upper reaches of the Chatanika River to gold dredges near Fairbanks owned by the Fairbanks Exploration Company (FE Company). The open canal section (83.5 miles total), with a width of 12-feet and depth of almost four-feet, was as large as some of the early tow-boat canals on the East Coast. But whoever coined the name for the system evidently liked alliteration and Davidson Ditch had more panache than Davidson Aqueduct.

Large-scale placer mining operations weren't considered feasible in Fairbanks before the 1920s because of the huge volumes of water needed and low seasonal water flow of local streams. For instance, Gold Dredge No. 8 used 9,000 gallons per minute, and five of the FE Company's dredges were supplied via the Davidson Ditch.

However, the same factors that allowed the FE Company to move into the Fairbanks area (opening of the Alaska Railroad and development of the Healy coal fields) also allowed mining engineers to develop large-scale waterworks necessary to make dredging profitable.

James Davidson, the mining engineer responsible for the 50-mile long Miocene Ditch on the Seward Peninsula, designed the Davidson Ditch. We talk about "green" technology now, but in 1925 the proposed aqueduct was as green as you could get. The entire system was gravity fed — no pumps.

From the containment dam just below Faith and McManus Creeks (southwest of 12-mile Summit) open ditches gradually descended along ridge lines. When the ditch reached a stream valley, inverted siphons made of 48- to 56-inch diameter steel pipe (15 siphons total) channeled the water down across the stream and back up the opposite slope. The FE Company used pipe of varying diameter for the project to reduce shipping costs. Smaller diameter pipe was nested inside larger pipe for shipment to Alaska.

Thus was water brought to the Cleary Creek dredges at Chatanika. But the water was also destined for the Goldstream Valley and the final obstacle was the ridge at the head of Vault Creek just north of Fairbanks. Too high to bring a ditch across, a 3,700-foot long tunnel was blasted though the ridge's crest.

According to John Boswell's book, *History of Alaskan Operations of United States Smelting, Refining and Mining Company*, work on the ditch began in 1924 and ended by 1928. Construction required steam and diesel shovels, tractors and graders, and plenty of handwork. (The steam shovels used came from the Panama Canal project.) The FE Company operated the ditch until 1958 when it began reducing its Fairbanks operations.

Photographs and supporting information in the Archives at the University of Alaska, Fairbanks indicate that ownership of the ditch was transferred to the Chatanika Power Company (CPC) in 1958. The CPC built a small hydroelectric plant at Chatanika and provided electricity to Fairbanks during summers from 1959 to 1967. In 1967 the same torrential rains that flooded Fairbanks also caused extensive damage to the Davidson Ditch's containment dam and the system was abandoned.

Much of the project's steel pipe has been removed, but portions of the ditch still exist within the Bureau of Land Management's White Mountains National Recreation Area north of the Steese Highway. A few of the siphons are easily visible, such as the one (shown in the drawing) that crosses U.S. Creek at Mile 57.5 of the highway.

Sources:

- *History of Alaskan Operations of United States Smelting, Refining and Mining Company*. John C. Boswell. Mineral Industry Research Laboratory. University of Alaska, Fairbanks. 1979
- "Chatanika Power Company Photographs." University of Alaska Fairbanks, Archives
- "Digging the Davidson: An engineering marvel," in *Heartland Magazine*. Jo Anne Wold, *Fairbanks Daily News-Miner*. July 14, 1984
- "The Davidson Ditch." Larry Gedney. Alaska Science Forum. August 29, 1983

Steese Highway, Central

Cariole sled at Central as it would have looked in 1900. Dog houses are typical of ones used during that time period

Museum at Central displays early dog sled development

The Circle District Historical Society Museum in Central, Alaska has several lovely old dog sleds on display, including some that would be familiar to most Alaskans—"basket" sleds with runners. But one very different type of sled, what might be described as a flat-sterned snow-canoe, caught my eye the first time I visited the museum.

About 11 feet long and only 18 inches wide, it has an upturned front end like a toboggan, is flat-bottomed, has form-fitted canvas sides, a canvas covering over its prow, and a backboard with back-sweeping handles. The drawing shows this freight-style toboggan as it would have looked at the beginning of the 1900s.

This is what Canadian fur traders called a "cariole," developed from the traditional Indian toboggan for the needs of the "voyageurs," and businesses like the Hudson's Bay Company.

Toboggans, used by Indians throughout the boreal forest stretching across the northern regions of North America, were ideally suited for winter travel through deep powder snow.

At their simplest, they were long narrow pieces of birch bark with wooden cross-pieces, lashed together with babiche (lacings made from sinew or rawhide), much as Jack London described in his book, *White Fang*. The prow of the toboggan was curved back (to deflect snow) and lashed into place. Light in weight—these sleds essentially floated on top of the snow and were narrow so they would fit within the track of a man on snowshoes.

As the sleds developed, wooden planks replaced the birch bark. Birch and ash were commonly used—the prows steamed and bent into shape.

Early fur traders took the basic toboggan and refined the design to meet their needs, adding a backboard and rawhide or canvas sides so the sled could carry additional cargo, and introducing dogs to pull the sleds. In the more "civilized" areas of Canada a covering was often added to the front half of the cariole so passengers could ride comfortably.

The Hudson's Bay Company carried this sled design across Canada and into Alaska, establishing a trading post in 1846 at Fort Yukon. Throughout Canada, local inhabitants adapted the cariole design to their own needs.

Thomas Swan, a musher in Two Rivers, Alaska, and local authority on toboggan-style sleds, says it was here in Alaska that the two basic types of dogsleds (toboggans and basket sleds) began to influence each other.

The Russian-American Company had established a trading post at Nulato (on the Lower Yukon River) in 1839. Its employees pushed further up the Yukon River on seasonal trading trips, and were well-aware of the British presence at Fort Yukon. The Russians used Siberian-influenced basket sleds for winter excursions, so it was there on the middle Yukon that the two sled-building traditions met.

However, it wasn't until after the popularization of mushing by arctic explorers such as Fridtjof Nansen and Robert Peary (who used Inuit-influenced basket sleds) and the North American gold rushes at the end of the 19th century that basket sleds began to overtake toboggan-type sleds in popularity.

Westerners pushing into Interior Alaska and the Klondike established regular winter trails frequented by freighters and mail carriers. On these packed trails, sleds with runners were faster and could haul more than flat-bottomed toboggans. Soon people began racing basket sleds, increasing their popularity.

Toboggans were still superior when operated off established trails and in deep snow, so remained useful. Hudson Stuck (Episcopal Archdeacon for Alaska) mentioned in his book *Ten Thousand Miles with a Dog Sled*, that in the early 1900s many Indians still used toboggans.

Toboggan-style sleds have seen a resurgence in popularity by subsistence users and recreationists since the 1960s, but the cariole design is all but lost.

Sources:

- Conversation with Thomas Swan, musher based in Two Rivers, Alaska
- "Marche, Sled Dogs in the Northwest Fur Trade," & "Stardancer Mushing Equipment." Thomas Swan. Stardancer Historical Freight Dogs website, no date
- "The Inuit Dog; Its provenance, environment and history." Ian MacRury. Master's Degree thesis at University of Cambridge. 1991
- *Ten Thousand Miles with a Dog Sled*. Hudson Stuck. C. Scribner's Sons. 1914
- *The World of Sled Dogs*. Lorna Coppinger. Howell Book House. 1977

Steese Highway, Circle Hot Springs

Circle Hot Springs in 2011

A haunting end to life at Circle Hot Springs

For countless generations before Westerners entered Interior Alaska, only Athabascan Indians used the hot springs located on the northeastern edge of the Tanana-Yukon Uplands, near where Birch Creek meandered out into the Yukon River lowlands. Then, in the 1890s, gold was discovered in the region and prospectors scattered into the hills in search of the motherlode.

Circle City (now just called Circle) was established on the south bank of the Yukon River in 1893 to supply the mining camps in the Birch Creek area about 50 miles to the southwest. (Miners erroneously thought the town was on the Arctic Circle, which is actually about 40 miles to the north.)

A roadhouse was built along the trail at Central, about 35 miles from Circle. Then, in the fall of 1893 a prospector named William Greats stumbled on the springs while hunting moose about eight miles southeast of Central.

Other prospectors quickly learned of the Arctic Circle hot springs and began spending their winters there. A 2007 publication, *The Healing Waters of Circle Hot Springs*, states that visitors at first lived in tents, but heavy ice build-up on the tent flaps was a constant problem so they began building cabins. In 1905 Cassius Monohan homesteaded 106 acres around the springs, and Franklin and Emma Leach bought the homestead from Monohan in 1909.

According to the *Alaska Community Database* maintained by the Alaska Department of Community and Regional Affairs, the Alaska Road Commission (ARC) began building a wagon road from Circle to the mining camps in 1906, and by 1908 the road had reached Central. The ARC completed the road to Fairbanks in 1927, and in 1930 the Leaches decided to build a hotel at the hot springs.

They hired local sourdough Billy Bowers to oversee construction, and work on the hotel begun in March 1930. Some accounts say most construction materials came by river to Circle and then by wagon to the springs. However, in a 1973 taped interview, Emma Leach said the logs used for lumber were felled at Medicine Lake several miles northeast of the springs, and that additional lumber was trucked from Fairbanks. The hotel was completed by that fall.

The hotel itself has changed little over the years and for the most part kept its rustic charm. The bay windows on the first floor can be seen in photos from the 1930s and 1940s, and appear to be original features. The only significant changes are the addition of a restaurant at the rear, and a front entry vestibule.

Until the 1950s the hot springs pool remained in a relatively natural state. A 1947 photograph shows the grass-fringed pool with a few Adirondack-style chairs along the edge, and a diving board at the pool's far end. Other early photographs show expansive gardens and several greenhouses to the right of the hotel (where the pool and other buildings are now).

Frank Leach died in 1955, and Emma managed the hotel until her death in 1974. They are both buried in a small cemetery (which contains about three dozen graves) on the hill above the hotel. In 1980 Bobby and Laverna Miller purchased the hotel and hot springs, which remained open until 2002.

In its heyday Circle Hot Springs attracted visitors from all over Alaska and beyond, and was well-known for its aurora viewing. The hotel supposedly even has its own ghost. Some employees are reported to have seen or felt the specter of Emma Leach roaming the halls or haunting the kitchen.

The hotel and hot springs are now closed and the property is for sale. Most of the land around the hot springs is private. You can drive by and see the hotel, but get permission before wandering around the property.

Sources:

- *Alaska Community Database*. Alaska State Department of Community and Regional Affairs. 2013
- "Emma Leach is interviewed by Mike Dalton in Central, Alaska on August 1973" (sound recording). University of Alaska Fairbanks, Oral History Collection
- "It's Still the Water at Circle." Dermot Cole. *Fairbanks Daily News-Miner.* No date,
- Photos of Circle Hot Springs, from Crystal & Ray Williams Photo Album. University of Alaska Anchorage, Archives
- Photos of Circle Hot Springs, from Leland A. Olson papers. University of Alaska Anchorage, Archives
- *Roadside Geology of Alaska*. Cathy Connor & Daniel O'Hare. Mountain Press Publishing. 1988
- *The Healing Water of Circle Hot Springs*. University of Alaska, Anchorage. LitSite Alaska website. 2006

Chena Hot Springs Road, Chena Hot Springs

Historic cabins at Chena Hot Springs in 1996

Find memories, welcome and soothing waters at Chena Hot Springs

Most Westerners exploring the Chena River drainage in the early 1900s had gold fever and were looking to get rich. Robert Swan had rheumatism and was just looking to ease his aching body.

He and his brother Tom were Fairbanks miners, but they heard about a U.S. Geological Survey party that had been working on the Upper Chena in 1904. The survey crew had seen steam rising from a valley somewhere ahead of them. Although they did not investigate, the workers thought there might be hot springs in the area.

In the summer of 1905 the two Swan brothers headed up the Chena with a boat-load of supplies. Over a month later they discovered hot springs about 60 miles northeast of Fairbanks on Monument Creek, a tributary of the North Fork of the Chena River. Supposedly they also found an old campfire ring that Felix Pedro had used.

When the Swans returned to Fairbanks, rejuvenated by the hot springs, other sore and weary residents headed there as well. George Wilson arrived at the springs and liked them so much he homesteaded the site in 1906, developing it as a health spa for Interior residents. By 1911 the spa's facilities consisted of a bathhouse, stable and 12 small log cabins. (The drawing shows the two surviving cabins from that period.)

Fairbanks residents were proud of their little home-grown spa, and in 1912 James Wickersham, who was by then Alaska's delegate to Congress, asked the U.S. Department of Agriculture to analyze the hot springs' water. The government's analysis showed the water was very similar to that of hot springs in Karlsbad, Bohemia (present day Karlovy Vary, Czech Republic).

Perhaps buoyed by this information, local residents petitioned the territorial government to get a road to the springs constructed. The Alaska Road Commission punched through a winter trail from Fairbanks to the hot springs in 1913. It had originally planned on constructing a regular road, but with short funding, a trail was the best that could be accomplished.

Today it takes less than two hours to reach Chena Hot Springs from Fairbanks via the paved year-round Chena Hot Springs Road (CHSR), but in the early 1900s it was at least a four-day journey. To serve the hot-springs-bound travelers three roadhouses were built: Little Chena Roadhouse (14-mile CHSR), Colorado Creek Roadhouse (near 32-mile CHSR), and Greg's Roadhouse (48-mile CHSR).

Much has changed over the years. With the construction of the road to the springs, the old roadhouses (no longer needed) were bypassed and fell into ruin. Development along the road increased, but fortunately, the State of Alaska set aside over 250,000 acres along the Upper Chena as the Chena River State Recreation Area. Chena Hot Springs is just outside the park's northeast boundary.

The water from the springs has been diverted and channeled numerous times, just as the building housing the in-door pool has been rebuilt and modified many times. But the water still bubbles up out of the ground at about 110 degrees Fahrenheit. (It has to be cooled down before entering the indoor pool.)

All the old buildings except for the two small 10' x 10' cabins (across the path from the pool building) have disappeared. Other than the cabins, the oldest building at the springs is the original portion of the main lodge and restaurant, constructed in 1939.

Numerous other buildings, including lodging units, smaller cabins, greenhouses and dog kennels have sprung up, but Chena Hot Springs still retains its rustic charm. And there is really nothing quite like floating in the large outdoor hot springs pool while the air temperature hovers around -40° Fahrenheit and the Northern Lights dance overhead.

Sources:

- Bureau of Land Management land records
- "Chena Hot Springs," in *Geo-Heat Center Bulletin*, Volume 27, No. 3. John Lund. Sept. 2006
- "History of Chena Hot Springs." Chena Hot Spring Resort website, 2012
- Fairbanks North Star Borough land records
- *Historic Resources in the Fairbanks North Star Borough*. Janet Matheson & Bruce Haldeman, 1981
- *History of the Chena River State Recreation Area*. Alaska Department of Natural Resources brochure. 2009

Fairbanks - Downtown, Cushman Street

Old City Hall in 2011

Old City Hall part of downtown Fairbanks modernization

By the 1930s, residents of Fairbanks were fed up with the fires that plagued downtown. In its short life, the city had already experienced major conflagrations in 1906 and 1919 that had consumed most of the district, plus numerous other building fires such as the Nordale Hotel fire in 1924. Consequently, in the latter 1920s the city began requiring downtown businesses to build "fireproof" structures.

Austin "Cap" Lathrop was the first to experiment with poured concrete buildings when he built the Empress Theater on Second Avenue in 1927 (now the Co-op Plaza). The Federal Court and Post Office building, completed in 1933, used the same technique. The city's school was destroyed in a December 1932 fire and was succeeded by the concrete Main School.

So it was understandable that when Fairbanks' residents decided the city's wood-frame firehouse had to be replaced the new building would be concrete. Henry W. Bittman, a prominent Seattle engineer and architect was selected to design the structure. Bittman was involved with design and construction of many Northwest landmarks, including the Olympic Tower and King County Courthouse in Seattle, and the Monte Cristo Hotel in Everett.

Bittman's design, a two-story building combining fire and police stations and City Hall, was constructed at the corner of Cushman Street and Fifth Avenue in 1935. The building (now called Old City Hall) has an art deco influence, with its emphasis on symmetry, rectilinear design, parallel lines and right angles, repeated low relief geometrical decoration and stepped-back structural elements. A belt of incised design encircles the structure below a parapet decorated with raised medallions. The corners of the building, with their vertically stacked grooves, mimic stone.

It fits in nicely with the Federal Courthouse and Main School (both art deco buildings located along Cushman Street). The three buildings anchored the downtown area and represented the city's transition from a rough-and-tumble frontier town to a more settled, refined city.

According to the National Register of Historic Places, the Old City Hall as originally constructed was 50 feet long and 48 feet deep. A large ground-level bay for fire equipment was located to the right of the centrally located Cushman Street entrance. A smaller bay was located at the rear of the building off Fifth Avenue.

The city clerk's office was in the southeast corner of the first floor. City Council chambers and the police and fire department offices, kitchen, dormitory and equipment rooms were on the second floor.

A 24-foot by 36-foot extension (to house additional fire equipment and offices) was constructed at the rear of the building in the 1940s. The extension also utilized poured concrete and matched the original's design. It was set back from the street to allow access to the rear equipment bay.

After the disastrous 1967 Chena River flood a new police and fire station was constructed several blocks away. The City continued to use Old City Hall for administrative offices, and the newly-freed space was converted into additional office space. The major exterior changes noticeable from Cushman Street were replacing the wooden fire equipment bay doors (to the right of the Cushman Street front entrance) with a new wood-frame wall containing two windows. Exterior door and windows were also updated.

In 1994, the City Council moved city offices into the Main School Building. For a time the City leased Old City Hall to the Downtown Association of Fairbanks and the Fairbanks Community Museum. The building was placed on the National Register of Historic Places in 2002.

The City sold Old City Hall in 2014, and it re-opened in 2016 as Fairbanks Distilling Company. The distillery's owners are committed to maintaining the historic authenticity of the building. As part of their efforts they have replicated the original fire-engine-bay doors, bringing the building's exterior closer to how it originally looked..

Sources:

- *American Architecture since 1789.* Marcus Whiffen. Massachusetts Institute of Technology. 1969
- *Buildings of Alaska.* Alison K. Hoagland. Oxford University Press. 1993
- *Fairbanks, a City Historic Building Survey.* Janet Matheson. City of Fairbanks. 1985
- *Fairbanks, A Pictorial History.* Claus M. Naske & Ludwig Rowinski. The Donning Company Publishers. 1981
- "Henry W. Bittman." Alan Michelson. Pacific Coast Architecture Database website, <https://pcad.lib.washington.edu/> 2005-2013
- "Old City Hall National Register of Historic Places Registration Form." Janet Haigh. National Park Service. 2001

Fairbanks - Downtown, 2nd Avenue

Lacey Street Theater in 1993

The Fairbanks Lacey Street Theater, grand building on a budget

Architectural historian Alison Hoagland, author of *Buildings of Alaska*, writes that the Lacey Street Theater, "is the finest Art Deco building in Fairbanks." The theater main entrance has graced the corner of Lacey Street and Second Avenue since Cap Lathrop built it in 1939.

The Lacey actually spans the end of the block between First and Second Avenues and is 53 feet wide by 143 feet long. It is a two-story concrete building with a small four-story stepped tower at the corner. When it was built is had a seating capacity of 540.

The theater was gutted by a fire in 1966, but was quickly rebuilt and refurbished. Within three months it was open again. Additional interior work was accomplished during the 1970s.

Throughout its history though, the theater's exterior has remained virtually unchanged. The building has horizontal banding stretching the length of its facade, with incised geometrical designs between the windows. The design elements are repeated on the tower.

My drawing shows the side entrance on Lacey Street, and the main entrance (with theater marquee) is around the corner on Second Avenue. There is also a door at the corner, but that entrance originally led to a bank occupying the corner space.

Benjamin Priteca, a leading architect in the Pacific Northwest, designed the Lacey. According to his listing in the *Pacific Coast Architecture Database,* Priteca was one of the premier theater architects of his day and designed over 150 theaters. Some of the theaters he designed include the Coliseum in Seattle, the Pantages in downtown Los Angeles and the Orpheum in San Francisco.

Austin E. "Cap" Lathrop hired Priteca to design the Lacey Street Theater and the Fourth Avenue Theater in Anchorage. Priteca lived in Seattle where Lathrop had connections, but Lathrop might have been more influenced in selecting Priteca because of Alexander Pantages, the vaudeville and theater mogul. Pantages had numerous theaters across the United States and Canada, and Priteca was Pantages' favorite architect.

I don't know if Lathrop and Pantages ever actually met, but Pantages did have Alaska connections. He came north in the Klondike gold rush and got his start as a theatrical entrepreneur in Dawson and Nome before moving to Seattle in 1902.

The book, *Alaska's First Homegrown Millionaire,* relates that Lathrop was an Alaska industrialist and entrepreneur. He began his Alaska ventures in 1895 when he and several partners bought a small two-masted auxiliary sailboat (a boat rigged as a sailboat but also having an inboard engine) and sailed it into Alaska waters just in time to take advantage of the lucrative Klondike gold rush.

Lathrop went on to invest in coal mines, banks, radio stations and other commercial enterprises, including a string of theaters in Cordova, Valdez, Anchorage and Fairbanks.

In addition to the Lacey Street Theater, he also constructed the Empress Theater just down the street. In 1924 Cap produced the first motion picture filmed entirely in Alaska, "The Cheechakos."

The Lacey operated as a movie theater for over 40 years, but it finally closed its doors in 1983. The building sat vacant for several years but was purchased in 1992 by Dick and Hoa Brickley. They re-opened it as the Fairbanks Ice Museum, which is still in business.

Pantages supposedly liked Priteca because the architect could create the appearance of opulence without spending exorbitantly. Pantages is credited with saying, "Any fool can make a place look like a million dollars by spending a million dollars, but it's not everybody who can do the same thing with half a million." I don't know how much Lathrop spent to build the Lacey, but it certainly looks like a million-dollar building to me.

Sources:

- *Alaska's first homegrown millionaire : life and times of Cap Lathrop.* Elizabeth A. Tower. Publication Consultants. 2006
- *American Architecture since 1789.* Marcus Whiffen. Massachusetts Institute of Technology. 1969
- "Alexander Pantages," *in Murray's People, a Collection of Essays.* Murray Morgan. Tacoma Public Library. 1960
- "Benjamin Priteca." Alan Michelson. *Pacific Coast Architecture Database,* University of Washington. *2005-2013*
- *Buildings of Alaska.* Alison K. Hoagland. Oxford University Press. 1993
- Conversation with Dick Brickley, current owner of building
- *Fairbanks, a City Historic Building Survey.* Janet Matheson. City of Fairbanks. 1985
- "Lacey Street Theatre, National Register of Historic Places - Registration Form." Russ Sackett, National Park Service, 1990

Fairbanks - Downtown, 1st Avenue

Pioneer Hotel in 1910

Pioneer Hotel no longer stands, but history remains

The Pioneer Hotel on First Avenue (where the Bridgewater hotel is now) was one of the landmarks in early Fairbanks. Located on the waterfront a half-block west of the Northern Commercial Company (NC Company), it grew along with Fairbanks.

In 1904 it was the Pioneer Bar, a two-story log building with the bar on the first floor, and perhaps rental rooms on the second floor. Within two years the bar had become secondary to the hotel. A false-front facade replaced bare logs, and the hotel's distinguishing features throughout its life were the bay windows installed on the second floor facing the river. The hotel gradually expanded into neighboring buildings, always adding bay windows on the second floor.

By the mid-1910s it was the premier hotel in Fairbanks. An ad in the 1915-16 edition of the *Alaska Gazetteer and Directory* (an annual publication highlighting communities and businesses across the state) described the Pioneer Hotel as the "largest, best equipped and most up-to-date hotel in the North." It boasted of the hotel's 100 rooms, bar, private offices, telephone room, billiard room, steam heat, electric lights and ... flush toilets. The ad went on to say the hotel also had a steam-heated stable, dog houses and sleigh storage.

It became the place for visiting dignitaries to stay. President Harding roomed there on his trip to Fairbanks in 1923, and aviator Wiley Post, along with humorist Will Rogers, overnighted at the Pioneer in 1936 before their ill-fated flight to Barrow. The hotel survived until 1952, when it was destroyed by fire.

The Pioneer Hotel was an integral part of the Chena River waterfront, and in the drawing (which shows the hotel as it looked in the mid-1910s) a corner of the Pioneer Dock can be seen in the lower left corner. The Pioneer Dock (constructed in 1906) was adjacent to the Northern Commercial Company Dock and served the North American Transportation and Trading Company (NAT&TC). The NAT&TC was the main rival to the NC Company-affiliated Northern Navigation Company.

Obviously, the waterfront in those early years looked much different than it does now. The NC and Pioneer Docks dominated the area between Cushman and Wickersham Streets. According to the Alaska Department of Transportation report, *Historical Development of the Chena River Waterfront,* the river banks (which had been stripped of vegetation) were prone to erosion and collapse due to frequent flooding, and residents attempted to stabilize the banks in numerous ways.

Revetments (retaining walls) of vertical logs were constructed, primarily near the NC and Pioneer docks, but also upriver to the far end of the business district. In other areas pilings were driven at the water's edge and brush and other debris sandwiched behind the piling. The covered docks disappeared in the 1920s (after the demise of steamboating) and the NC power plant then dumped its ash and clinkers over the riverbank to stabilize it.

Most of those early efforts at riverbank containment have disappeared, replaced by rip-rap. However, if you know where to look, such as just upstream from the Wendell Street Bridge near Graehl Park, you can still see vestiges of the old waterfront — scattered stumps of pilings, and collapsed sections of log revetment peeking out from under willows and grasses along the shore.

Sources:

- *Alaska Gazetteer and Directory*. R. L. Polk & Company. 1915-16
- *Fairbanks, a City Historic Building Survey*. Janet Matheson. City of Fairbanks. 1985
- *Historical development of the Chena River Waterfront, Fairbanks, Alaska*. Pete Bowers and Brian Gannon. Alaska Department of Transportation and Public Facilities. 1998
- *Historic Fairbanks*. Dermot Cole. Historical Publishing Network. 2002
- Photo of Pioneer Hotel in early 1900s, from Albert Johnson Photo Collection. University of Alaska Fairbanks, Archives

Fairbanks - Downtown, 1st Avenue

Masonic Temple in 1996

Fairbanks' historic Masonic Temple is no more

One of the most iconic buildings along the Fairbanks riverfront, the 112-year-old Masonic Temple at 809 First Ave., was demolished on March 17, 2018 after a portion of the roof collapsed. So died a unique piece of Alaska history dating back to the founding of Fairbanks.

Fraternal organizations were popular in Alaska's fledgling towns. The Arctic Brotherhood, Eagles, Elks, Freemasons, Moose and Odd Fellows were all represented.

According to the 1921 edition of "Mackey's History of Freemasonry," by the 1920s seven chartered Masonic lodges existed in Alaska. Freemasonry arrived in Fairbanks soon after the city's founding, and although the local chapter (Tanana Lodge) did not receive its charter until 1908, the men who started the lodge were active Masons before the local chapter was officially recognized.

National Register of Historic Places documents

state that the building that became the Freemasons' home was constructed in 1906 as the Tanana Commercial Company store. Two years later the Masonic Lodge purchased the structure. The Masons added a basement and constructed an extension to the rear and a second story.

In 1916, the lodge undertook a major renovation and a pressed metal façade was installed over the front of the building, giving it a Renaissance Revival appearance. (Renaissance Revival is an architectural style inspired by various classical Italian styles.)

Pressed metal ornamentation and facades were extremely popular during the early 1900s, and there were thousands of buildings across the U.S. and Canada with pressed metal exteriors. The facades were a quick and inexpensive way to add style to otherwise plain buildings. Pressed metal could mimic brick, stone and concrete, as well as intricate floral and other decorative motifs.

Old catalogs indicate that a metal façade for the Masonic temple would have cost about $665 (plus shipping) in 1916. The inflation-adjusted price today would be about $16,000.

Some buildings in Skagway, Juneau and other Alaska towns have pressed metal decorative elements such a cornices and windows, but as far as I know, this Fairbanks building was the only structure in Alaska with an entirely-metal front façade. (Dawson City's Masonic Temple also has a pressed metal façade.)

The Masonic Temple was one of the civic centers in early Fairbanks, and numerous community events were held there. When President Warren Harding visited Fairbanks in 1923, he addressed city residents from the front steps of the Temple.

Local Masons were justly proud of the building, and the temple was listed on the National Register of Historic Places in 1980.

However, the cost to bring it up to modern building codes eventually became too expensive for the lodge, and the Masons decided to sell the building. Local businessman Harold Groetsema (former owner of Big Daddy's BarB-Q across the street) purchased the building in 2009 with the hope of turning the first floor into a banquet hall.

Harold told me that after beginning renovations he uncovered some interesting architectural details. For instance, ceiling sprinklers had been installed in the main hall and a suspended ceiling put in to hide the pipes. Tearing into the ceiling he discovered the original pressed metal ceiling tiles still in place. Unfortunately, Harold also found the cost of renovating and bring the building up to code to be cost-prohibitive. For the past decade the building sat mostly vacant, used only for storage.

Inadequately engineered from the start, it succumbed to old age and heavy snows. Its demise perhaps was inevitable, but it is a shame that the front façade was not salvaged so that the structure could be rebuilt. Only the pediment atop the building, inscribed with the words "Masonic Temple," and the date "1906," survived.

Sources:

• "A short history of Freemasonry in the Yukon", Jacques Boily. Grand Lodge of British Columbia and Yukon. 2002
• "Buildings of Alaska." Alison K. Hoagland. Oxford University Press. 1993
• Conversation with Harold Groetsema, current owner of old Masonic Temple property
• *Fairbanks, a City Historic Building Survey*. Janet Matheson. City of Fairbanks. 1985
• "Fairbanks Masonic Temple, National Register of Historic Places Inventory-Nomination Form." James R. Marcotte. National Park Service. 1979
• *Geo. L. Mesker & Co. Architectural Iron Works Catalog*. University of Houston Digital Library. C 1915
• Historic Masonic Temple total loss." Robin Wood. In *Fairbanks Daily News-Miner*. 3-18-2018
• *Mackey's History of Freemasonry*. Albert G. Mackey. Masonic History Company. 1921

Fairbanks - Downtown, 1st Avenue

Bathhouse in 2011

First Avenue bathhouse a home for many different groups

The simple but graceful two-story building at 815 First Avenue began life as the First Avenue Bath House.

In the early decades of the 1900s, indoor plumbing was a rarity in the Fairbanks area and hot baths were a luxury. A handful of bathhouses, including the one on First Avenue, sprang up in Fairbanks to serve the needs of the city's residents and the thousands of miners in the surrounding area.

According to the book, *This Old House, the Story of Clara Rust*, Cora Madole was the bathhouse's proprietor. (Rust was Madole's daughter.) Madole, also known as Madame Renio, had been a fortune teller in Dawson City during the Klondike gold rush, and moved to Fairbanks in 1903.

In 1906 she and her business partner, "Doc" Overgaard, built the bathhouse. The building consists of a small two-story section (about 12 feet by 18 feet) at the front of the structure and a long narrow (about 24 feet by 80 feet) one-story section stretching back the length of the lot. Madole's apartment was upstairs.

Doc Overgaard had a health clinic in the small first floor room fronting First Avenue and his apartment was tucked underneath the stairs. Doc evidently wasn't a real doctor. At least part of his "health clinic" income seems to have been derived from sobering up inebriated miners.

The rest of the building was devoted to the bathhouse. It had three bath stalls plus a steam room with a massage slab. Small rooms were located behind the bath stalls where customers could rest or even spend the night. At the rear of the building was a boiler shed.

Unfortunately, the bathhouse's water pipes froze during the winter of 1909-10 and Madole's business was forced to close.

The nomination form for the National Register of Historic Places states that The International Order of Odd Fellows (a benevolent, service-oriented organization) bought the building soon thereafter to use as its meeting hall, converting Doc's apartment into a bathroom, the front clinic into a kitchen and the rest of the first floor into a meeting and social room.

The Golden North Rebekah Lodge (a sister organization to the Odd Fellows) purchased the building in 1967. It removed the boiler shed on the back of the building, renovated the kitchen and remodeled the meeting room. From 2000 to 2003 the lodge replaced the badly deteriorated original foundation and the building's metal roof.

For over 90 years the Odd Fellows and Rebekah Lodges served the Fairbanks community from their First Avenue location, working on service projects, opening the building for community events and offering aid during local disasters.

Unfortunately, due to declining membership, the Rebekah Lodge closed its doors in 2007. Local businesswoman and history buff Candy Waugaman acquired the building from the Rebekah Lodge and subsequently organized a non-profit organization, Historic Hall Inc., to manage it. Waugaman, an inveterate collector, opened, and for several years operated, a museum in the building featuring Alaska memorabilia and ephemera.

Since Waugaman's museum closed a series of businesses have occupied the building. Waugaman sold the building in 2018 and it is now occupied by an antiques store, so it is still filled with memories and memorabilia.

Sources:

- *Buildings of Alaska*. Alison K. Hoagland. Oxford University Press. 1993
- Conversation with Candy Waugaman, who organized restoration of the building
- *Fairbanks, a City Historic Building Survey*. Janet Matheson. City of Fairbanks. 1985
- "Fairbanks Odd Fellows Hall, National Register of Historic Places Inventory-Nomination Form." David Libbey. National Park Service. 1979
- "Latest downtown museum to feature Alaska history." Dermot Cole. *Fairbanks Daily New-Miner*. July 12, 2013
- *This Old House, the Story of Clara Rust*. Jo Anne Wold. Alaska Northwest Books. 1989

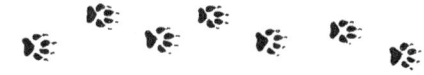

Fairbanks - Downtown, Cowles Street

The Falcon Joslin House in 2011

The Falcon Joslin House, vestige of a builder's dream

The Falcon Joslin House at 413 Cowles Street stands as testament to the determination of Falcon Joslin, the builder of the Tanana Valley Railroad and one of the earliest promoters of the Tanana Valley. It also marks the evolution of Fairbanks from a possibly temporary mining camp to a permanent community.

Falcon Joslin was born in Belleview, Tennessee in 1866, graduated from Vanderbilt University, and for a time practiced law in Seattle. When word of the Klondike gold strike reached Seattle, he joined the throngs of gold seekers headed north. In Dawson City, he organized the Dawson Electric and Power Company, and helped build the Coal

Creek railroad — a narrow-gauge railroad from the coal deposits on Coal Creek to the Yukon River (The power plant in Dawson City ran on coal).

As mining activity in the Klondike wound down, Joslin joined the exodus of miners to the Tanana Valley. Recognizing the need for reliable transportation between mining camps and the riverboat docks along the Chena River, he built (with American and English backing) the Tanana Mines Railroad — later called the Tanana Valley Railroad (TVRR).

Shortly after moving to Fairbanks in 1904, Joslin commissioned construction of a two-and-a-half-story wood frame house — one of the first wood frame houses in Fairbanks, and probably the oldest wood frame house still at its original location. Construction began in 1904 and was completed in 1905.

He built the large house to entice his wife and children to live in Fairbanks. However, for most of the time that he resided here, Joslin's family lived in Seattle and he rambled about the large house by himself.

Joslin's home is an example of "square built" houses found throughout the Midwest during that time period. Square built houses, also called foursquare or prairie square houses, were typically built on a square or nearly square floor plan, were usually at least two stories tall, had pyramidal or hipped roofs, large porches, dormers, and simple ornamentation. The Joslin house, with its shiplap siding, fulfills all these requirements.

Anywhere in the Lower 48, it might have fit in unobtrusively. In Fairbanks in 1905, the Joslin house stood in startling contrast to the temporary tents and simple log cabins that made up most of Fairbanks. But it, along with other houses such as that of Judge James Wickersham (also built in 1904), reflected the settling down of the city.

The city's changing nature did not bring Falcon Joslin peace, however. The TVRR prospered while gold production remained high, but after 1909, as drift mines closed and the area's population dwindled, the railroad suffered.

Joslin saw the potential for agricultural development in the Tanana Valley and he labored to expand the area's economic base to make up for the declining mining activity. His efforts perhaps had some effect, but they did not save the railroad.

The Fairbanks area's improving road system and competing trucking businesses eventually led to the railroad's demise. The Alaska Engineering Commission, which was building the Alaska Railroad from Seward to Fairbanks, acquired the TVRR in 1917. The year before that, Joslin sold his Fairbanks house and joined his family in Seattle. He died there in 1928.

The Fairbanks Exploration Company bought the Joslin house in 1923 to use as employee housing and added the single-room hipped roof addition on the north side of the house. Except for that and a garage addition at the rear of the house, the home is still remarkably close to its original condition. It was added to the National Register of Historic Places in 1980. It is now a private residence.

Sources:

- *Buildings of Alaska*. Alison K. Hoagland. Oxford University Press. 1993
- *Fairbanks, a City Historic Building Survey*. Janet Matheson. City of Fairbanks. 1985
- Fairbanks North Star Borough Land Records
- "Falcon Joslin House, National Register of Historic Places Inventory-Nomination Form." Robert Betts. National Park Service. 1979
- *Tanana Valley Railroad, the Gold Dust Line*. Nicholas Deely. Denali Designs. 1996

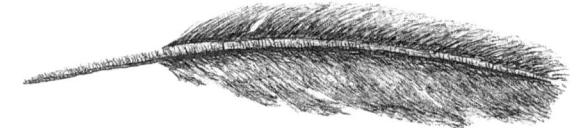

Fairbanks - Downtown, 1st Avenue

Thomas Memorial Library building in 1991

Thomas Memorial Library a civilizing influence in early Fairbanks

Fairbanks' first public library (pictured in the drawing) is a direct result of Episcopal Church efforts to provide reading materials for residents of Alaska's frontier settlements. The book, *O Ye Frost and Cold, a History of St. Matthew's Episcopal Church*, relates that Hudson Stuck, Episcopal Archdeacon of the Yukon, wrote in 1904 that there were few places in Fairbanks for men to go in the evening, "...save the saloons with their lewd pictures, their gambling tables and their general blackguardism."

St. Matthew's Church, like many other Episcopal missions in Alaska, offered an alternative by opening a reading room. After Sunday services a curtain was drawn in front of the chancel (the area around the altar). The nave (where the congregation sat) was then used as a reading room for the rest of the week. Every day and long into each evening, the room was crowded with men reading or writing letters. Regular appeals went out in national Episcopal publications for reading materials of all types, and residents all over the U.S. generously responded. Soon the reading room boasted 2000 books and multitudes of periodicals.

According to a 2009 *Fairbanks Daily News-Miner* article about the centennial of the Thomas Memorial Library, those appeals caught the attention of George C. Thomas, a Philadelphia banker who served as treasurer of the Domestic and Foreign Mission Society of the national Episcopal Church. In May 1909, Thomas donated $4,000 for construction of a library in Fairbanks and an additional $1,000 per year for three years' maintenance.

A 40-foot by 40-foot building was constructed that summer about a block east of the Episcopal Church, at 901 First Avenue. The library was built of 6-inch diameter logs (sawn flat on three sides) and had wide porches running the entire length of the north and east sides. A distinctive hipped roof, extending out over the porches, capped the structure, with small arched eye-brow dormer windows highlighting the roof over each porch.

In addition to serving Fairbanks, the reading room (and later the library) shipped bundles of periodicals all over Interior Alaska. In 1912 the Rev. Louis H. Bulsch wrote:, "Wherever one may choose to travel in the Interior, it matters not how remote the camp may be, he is sure to see magazines and papers bearing the mission's stamp. If you should visit a miner's cabin in the foothills of Mt. McKinley, in the Koyukuk, in the Birch or Beaver diggings, during the long winter nights you would invariably find that his reading material has come from St. Matthew's."

Although it may not have seemed important at the time, a significant event in Alaska history occurred at the library on July 5, 1915. On that day six Tanana village chiefs met with representatives of the federal government to discuss Native lands and maintaining the Athabascans' traditional lifestyle. This was perhaps the first conference held concerning Alaska Native land claims.

St. Matthew's turned the library over to the City of Fairbanks in 1942 and the building served as the City library until 1968 when the Fairbanks North Star Borough assumed ownership. After Noel Wien Library was built in 1977, the Borough sold the old library building. It has changed ownership several times since then, and John and Ramona Reeves currently have title to it

The former library's interior has been extensively modified over time, but the original pressed-tin paneling can still be seen on a few walls. The exterior showed more modest changes, and the Reeves have now restored the exterior to its original configuration.

In 1972, the site was listed in the National Register of Historic Places, and in 1978 it became a National Historic Landmark.

Sources:

- *Buildings of Alaska*. Alison K. Hoagland. Oxford University Press. 1993
- *Fairbanks, a City Historic Building Survey*. Janet Matheson. City of Fairbanks. 1985
- Fairbanks North Star Borough property records
- "George C. Thomas Memorial Library is 100 years old." Tom Alton. *Fairbanks Daily News-Miner.* August 7, 2009
- "George C. Thomas Memorial Library, National Register of Historic Places Inventory-Nomination Form." John Antonson, National Park Service. 1976
- *O Ye frost and Cold, a history of St. Matthew's Episcopal Church.* Arnold Griese and Ed Bigelow. St. Matthew's Episcopal Church. 1980

Fairbanks - Downtown, 1st Avenue

St. Matthew's Church in 1992

St. Matthew's Episcopal Church retains its rustic charm

When Episcopal Bishop Peter Trimble Rowe mushed into Fairbanks in February 1904, he found a certified boom-town. The previous March, an Episcopal priest had visited the gold camp (mushing from the Episcopal mission at Circle City), but found only E. T. Barnette's store, a partially-constructed two-story log hotel, two saloons, a half-dozen rough cabins and a few tents.

The book, *O Ye Frost and Cold, a History of St. Matthew's Episcopal Church*, tells that the earlier priest, the Reverend Charles E. Rice, under-awed by Fairbanks and its prospects, held church services and promptly returned to Circle City. What a difference a year made. Bona fide big gold strikes were made on several creeks in the fall of 1903, and by 1904 Fairbanks had several thousand residents.

Bishop Rowe was warmly welcomed, and with the encouragement and financial support of Fairbanks residents, set in motion efforts that culminated in the building of St. Matthew's Church and hospital.

The Episcopal Church knew that Fairbanks lacked a hospital and began work that spring on St. Matthew's Hospital, which was to be a 30 foot by 50 foot two-story wood-frame structure. According to the book, *Fairbanks, a City Historic Building Survey*, the hospital building was probably one of the first frame buildings in Fairbanks.

The shell of the hospital was up by August, and by mid-September the building was finished enough to admit patients. Unfortunately, by the end of the month the hospital was already overcrowded. (In 1906 the Catholic Church built St. Joseph's hospital across the Chena River, and St. Matthew's hospital closed in 1915.) It is somewhat telling of the Episcopal mission's priorities that St. Matthew's Church was not started until after the hospital was completed.

Work on the church began Sept. 26, 1904 and the first service was held October 16. The church was a 40-foot by 25-foot log building constructed of rough logs with the bark still on. Typical of other Episcopal churches in Interior Alaska, it had a vestibule (entry), and a belfry (bell tower) on the roof of the nave (main part of the church).

In February 1947 the church was seriously damaged in a fire. Parishioners were able to save the hand carved altar, lectern, altar rail and the original bell. Fortunately, plans to replace the church building had already begun. In 1946 the parish had realized the church structure was not in good condition and contracted with Bell and Upjohn Architects of New York City to design a new church.

Thomas Bell and Hobart Upjohn were well-known New York ecclesiastical architects and had already designed numerous churches (including Episcopal) up and down the East Coast. Hobart's father and grandfather were also architects. His grandfather, Richard Upjohn, introduced the Gothic Revival style to the U.S. and designed Trinity Church in New York City.

The new church was patterned after the original's simplicity. It was constructed of peeled logs sawn flat on three sides, and featured similar gable-fronted nave and vestibule. Two major differences in the new church were the more steeply pitched roof, and the belfry's location on top of the vestibule — tucked under the nave's roof. When the building was completed the altar, lectern, altar rail, and bell from the old church were re-installed. The first services in the new church were held on Christmas Eve, 1948. Additions have been made to the rear of the church, but the structure still retains its simple rustic beauty.

The church was added to the National Register of Historic Places in 2016.

Sources:

- *Buildings of Alaska*. Alison K. Hoagland. Oxford University Press. 1993
- *Fairbanks, a City Historic Building Survey*. Janet Matheson. City of Fairbanks. 1985
- "Hobart Brown Upjohn (1876-1949." Gerald Allen. *North Carolina Architects and Builders, a Biographical Dictionary* website. North Carolina State University. 2009
- *O Ye frost and Cold, a history of St. Matthew's Episcopal Church*. Arnold Griese and Ed Bigelow. St. Matthew's Episcopal Church. 1980

Fairbanks - Pioneer Park, Pioneer Museum

One of Ed Orr's
Fairbanks-Valdez Stages in 1999

Valdez-Fairbanks Trail, a lifeline for early Interior Alaskans

The Ed S. Orr Stage Company, also called the Fairbanks-Valdez Stage Company, was the most successful of several stage lines that operated along the Valdez-Fairbanks Trail between 1904 and the mid-1910s. One of his stages (now in the Pioneer Museum at Pioneer Park) is depicted in the drawing parked in front of a now-gone building on Dunkel Street that was used as a garage by Orr.

This route was an essential lifeline to Fairbanks (especially during the winter), but actually began as an offshoot of the Valdez-Eagle Trail (Trans-Alaska Military Road). According to *Alaska's Heritage,* an Alaska Humanities Forum publication, the Valdez-Eagle Trail was established by the U.S. government in response to the clamor for an all-American route from the ice-free waters of southern Alaska to the Yukon River and gold-fields of the Klondike.

It wound northwest from Valdez over Thompson Pass, north across the Copper River Valley to Gakona, and thence northwest across Mentasta Pass and on to Eagle. The trail was begun in 1899 and completed by 1901, but by the time it was finished the Klondike Gold Rush was dying down and gold would soon be discovered in the hills above the Chena River.

Gold seekers heading for Fairbanks began taking the Valdez-Eagle Trail as far as the Gakona River, then crossing Isabelle Pass to the north, and following the Delta River north and west into the Tanana River Valley. This route, following old Indian trails, would become the route for winter mail delivery between Fairbanks and Valdez, and later for pack trains and wagons.

Ken Marsh's book, *The Trail, the Story of the Historic Valdez-Fairbanks Trail,* relates that the Valdez Transportation Company was one of the pioneering stage companies in Interior Alaska. It began running pack trains and sleds over the Valdez-Fairbanks winter trail in 1904, and the next winter it was given a government contract to deliver the mail between Valdez and Fairbanks eight times a month, and to Tanana four times a month.

Also in 1904, the federal government recommended that the War Department build a system of trails in Alaska and upgrade the Valdez-Eagle Trail to a wagon Road. The Alaska Road Commission (ARC), headed by Capt. Wilds P. Richardson, was subsequently created to oversee Alaska's road and trail system.

The ARC quickly began improving the winter mail route from Fairbanks to Valdez, eventually linking the trail up with the Valdez-Eagle Trail. The improved winter trail out of Fairbanks was completed in 1907 and an all-season wagon road was completed by 1910.

Ed Orr was already an experienced freighter when he began the Fairbanks-Valdez Stage in 1906. He had run pack trains up the Chilkoot Trail out of Dyea in 1898, and operated a successful stage company out of Dawson City between 1899 and 1905. In his first year of business along the Valdez-Fairbanks Trail he beat out the Valdez Transportation Company for the mail contract.

The Valdez-Fairbanks Trail was about 360 miles long. Orr ran stages (equipped with wheels or runners depending on the season) 2-3 times a week out of both cities, and each stage took about eight days for a one-way trip. Since horses had to be changed every 20-25 miles, and the stages had to overnight every 40-50 miles, the numerous roadhouses along the route were essential. Orr built barns and other facilities at roadhouse stage stops all along the trail.

The Northern Commercial Company bought the stage line from Orr in 1910 and it continued to operate until 1914. By then newly formed automobile stage lines had taken much of the business away from horse-drawn stages.

Sources:

- *Alaska's Heritage, Chapter 4-10: Road transportation.* The Alaska History & Cultural Studies Website. Alaska Humanities Forum. 2004-2011
- *America's Territory, Overland Routes Develop.* The Alaska History & Cultural Studies Website. Alaska Humanities Forum. 2004-2011
- *Blazing Alaska's Trails.* Alfred Hulse Brooks. University of Alaska and Arctic Institute of North America. 1953
- *Roadhouses of the Richardson Highway.* Walter Phillips. Alaska Historical Commission. 1984
- *The Eagle-Valdez Trail – Northern Portion,* Bureau of Land Management, N.D.
- *The Trail, the Story of the Historic Valdez-Fairbanks Trail.* Kenneth Marsh. Trapper Creek Museum. 2008

Fairbanks - Pioneer Park, Gold Rush Town

The Lavelle Young in front of Barnette's Cache in 1904

Charles Adams and the SS Lavelle Young, icons of Alaska steamboating

Two riverboats are represented at Pioneer Park: the SS Lavelle Young (first commercial steamboat to navigate the Chena River in 1901), and the SS Nenana (last steamer to Fairbanks in 1957). In between many steamboats and steamboaters came and went, but one of the constants was Charles Adams. He was the majority owner of the Lavelle Young and was on board when E. T. Barnette chartered the boat in 1901. Later, Adams was appointed captain of the Nenana when it was launched in 1933.

According to his autobiography, *A Cheechako Goes to the Klondike*, before Adams became a steamboater he was a successful Klondike miner, and also participated in the Nome stampede. Returning from Nome, he and his partners (Tom Bruce and George Crummy) bought the Lavelle Young at St. Michael in 1900. None of the partners had steamboating experience, so they hired a captain and crew, with Bruce serving as steward and Adams as purser. (Adams eventually got his master's paper in 1908.)

In the summer of 1901, Barnette was eager to reach Tanana Crossing (present-day Tanacross) and establish a trading post. Unfortunately, his boat wrecked before clearing St. Michael harbor, so he chartered the Lavelle Young to run his supplies up the Tanana River.

Adams checked with more experienced river men who felt it unlikely the Lavelle Young could get beyond Chena Slough. (At that time the lowest section of the Chena River was actually part of a Tanana River slough that exited the main Tanana River channel upriver from Moose Creek Bluffs.

After negotiating with Barnette, Adams wisely inserted a provision in their contract stating that if the boat got beyond the mouth of Chena Slough but could go no further, Barnette and party would disembark wherever that spot was.

Sure enough, the Lavelle Young could not get past Bates Rapids on the Tanana River (just above the Chena). Barnette convinced Adams to try and bypass the rapids via Chena Slough but sandbars prevented them from progressing very far.

The boat lacked a capstan winch and Adams was hesitant to go back down the Chena with a fully loaded boat and risk getting hard stuck. So an unhappy Barnette, his business associates, crying wife, and all their goods were unloaded on a bank of the Chena. Thus was Fairbanks born. The drawing shows the Lavelle Young in front of Barnette's Cache in 1904.

Adams enjoyed a long career before retiring in 1942, but the Lavelle Young had a relatively short steamboat life. Built in 1898, she was 140 feet long, 32 feet wide, drew 3 feet of water, and was actually designed for clearing snags on the Columbia River. (She was named for the granddaughter of a prominent Oregon businessman.)

A 1909 book, *Through the Yukon and Alaska,* relates that the Lavelle Young was brought to Alaska to clear Koyukuk River channels, but diverted to the more lucrative passenger and freight trade.

Northern Navigation Company bought her from Adams and partners in 1903, moving the boat to the Kuskokwim River in 1910. She operated there a few years, but was considered too large and expensive to operate and was mothballed.

American-Yukon Navigation Company acquired Northern Navigation's fleet in 1914. It sold the Lavelle Young in 1920 to Alaska Rivers Navigation Company which converted her to a cold-storage barge.

The Lavelle Young was later abandoned, and sank around 1930. The Alaska Heritage Records Survey indicates the remains of her wheelhouse were found near McGrath in the 1970s. What was left of the wheelhouse was returned to Fairbanks and reconstructed by the Fairbanks Historical Preservation Foundation. It is now on display at Pioneer Park.

Sources:

- *A Cheechako Goes to the Klondike.* Charles W. Adams. Epicenter Press. 2003
- "Lavelle Young" entry, in *H. W. McCurdy Marine History of the Pacific Northwest.* Gordon R. Newell. Superior Publishing Company. 1966
- "Lavelle Young Riverboat Site Card." John Beck. Alaska Heritage Resource Survey. 1977
- Photo of Barnette's Cache in June of 1904, from Robert Jones Collection. University of Alaska Fairbanks, Archives
- Photo of Lavelle Young at Tanana from Falcon Joslin Papers. University of Alaska Fairbanks, Archives
- *Through the Yukon and Alaska.* Thomas Arthur Rickard. Mining and Scientific Press. 1909

Palace Hotel in 2011

Palace Hotel a rare survivor of Fairbanks early business district

The old Palace Hotel, a two-story log structure now located at Pioneer Park, is a rare survivor of Fairbanks' early business district. According to the City of Fairbanks and the Fairbanks North Star Borough Commission on Historic Preservation, it "is the last remaining multi-story log commercial building representing this early period of commercial development."

The front of the building is about 30 feet wide, and the sides are about 40 feet in length. The sides are composed of two sections, with both sections similar in construction and probably built at the same time. Janet Matheson, author of the book, *Fairbanks, a City Historic Building Survey*, surmises this method was used because longer logs were in short supply.

The two-story structure has numerous windows — all tall, narrow, double-hung windows. There are several different window types however, with some being single-pane, others having two panes and others with more. Speculation is that the structure may have been finished at the end of a building season with whatever windows were left at the local hardware store.

The log walls are tied together with vertical corner posts covered with trim boards. Two vertical log posts on either side of the building help support the roof, but whether these are original is unknown. The original roof was galvanized metal, which has been replaced with modern metal roofing.

Pretty much everything else about the building is original, however. The sides and rear of the building retain their original appearance, and the front of the building has changed little in 100 years. Early photos show that the double front door (now in the right corner) used to be a single door in the center of the front façade, and the center window used to be in the right front corner. (Aside from early photo evidence, you can surmise the door installation was done at a different date, since the cuts to the surrounding logs are at a steeper angle than around the windows.)

Although determining when the hotel was actually built is impossible, early records show it was located on Fourth Avenue, between Cushman and Lacey Street, in 1910. The year it was built can be dated earlier, though, based on building materials. The use of logs pushes its origin back to the town's early years, when logs were commonly used.

The devastating Fairbanks fire of 1906 leveled the four-block central section of the Fairbanks business district — from Turner to Lacey Street, and Front Street (First Avenue) to Third Avenue. Afterward, business buildings were constructed of sawn lumber, so the Palace Hotel's log construction probably dates it to at least 1906.

The building started off as the Palace Hotel but the name was later changed to the Palace Hotel and Bathhouse. It was near the Fourth Avenue gate allowing entrance to "The Line," (as the red light district was called) so it was probably a popular stopping place for miners coming in from the creeks.

In 1957 it became the Chena Hotel, and in 1967 the building was moved to Alaskaland (now Pioneer Park) as part of the A-67 Centennial Exposition celebrating the 100th anniversary of Alaska's purchase from Russia.

The building began life at Alaskaland as an example of a Northern Commercial Company store, and then became the Pantages Theater. (Alexander Pantages was an impresario who owned theaters across the Western Unites States and Canada. He got his theatrical start in Dawson City and Nome but never owned a theater in Fairbanks.) The building has been occupied by a variety of tenants over the years and is still one of the focal points of the park's Gold Rush Town.

Sources:

- *Historic Preservation Plan*. City of Fairbanks and Fairbanks North Star Borough Joint Commission on Historic Preservation. 2006
- *Fairbanks, a City Historic Building Survey*. Janet Matheson. City of Fairbanks. 1985
- Photo of Palace Hotel in early 1900s, from W. F. Erskine Collection, University of Alaska Fairbanks, Archives
- *Steamboats on the Chena, the Founding and Development of Fairbanks, Alaska*. Basil Hendricks & Susan Savage. Epicenter Press. 1988

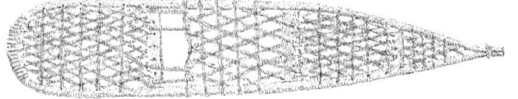

Fairbanks - Pioneer Park, Gold Rush Town

Kitty Hensley House in 1996

Pioneer Park house offers glimpse of mysterious Kitty Hensley

Kitty Hensley is a bit of a mystery. No one is quite sure when she came to Fairbanks, when she married, or who exactly her husband was. Some say he was a lawyer from Nome, but no one is sure. We do know from records at the Kitty Hensley House that she was born Katherine Kilway in Michigan in 1867. She left home at an early age and by the

1880s she was in California, working on riverboats and in dance halls and saloons.

When gold was discovered in the Yukon and Alaska, she ventured north. It is unknown whether she came as a working single girl or as Mrs. Hensley. What is known is that by 1903 she was married and living in a small cabin on Eighth Avenue.

Her husband evidently owned the Florence S, a small steamboat. But Mr. Hensley abandoned both his wife and steamboat in the early 1900s. After Kitty's husband disappeared, she became owner of the Florence S, while E. J. Smythe, who was captain at the time, maintained control.

A publication entitled *Yukon Riverboat Captains*, by Jerry Green, states that Smythe sailed north from Olympia, Washington when word of the Klondike gold rush reached the West Coast. He traversed the Chilkoot Trail in July of 1898, and immediately began skippering riverboats on the Yukon River. Smythe spent five years on the upper Yukon before moving to Fairbanks as skipper of the Florence S.

According to folklore, Kitty traveled aboard the Florence S for a time while Smythe was captain, but her eccentric character and headstrong will clashed with that of the crew and captain. Complaints from the crew forced Smythe to banish Kitty from the boat in 1910.

After that Kitty stayed in Fairbanks. Several years later Smythe was returning to Fairbanks on the last run of the season when low water in the Chena River prevented him from reaching safe winter moorage. The Florence S spent the winter frozen into the Tanana River ice, and breakup the next spring damaged the boat beyond repair.

Smythe salvaged lumber and fixtures from the boat, and used some of the salvage to remodel Kitty's home. Kitty's original cabin was constructed of logs squared on three sides and mitered at the corners. Smythe added a second story, replacing the cabin's simple gable roof with a gambrel roof having two slopes on each side.

A porch and small room were added to the front of the house, topped with a sloping concave roof. The house was roofed with wood shingles, and the front of the house was also sheathed with wood shingles in varying shapes and patterns.

Smythe styled the remodeled house after the Queen Anne cottages popular in the Lower 48. He installed fancy windows (the upper sashes in each window were outlined with red glass squares and frosted-glass rectangles) and topped the bedroom window in the second floor with an arch.

The captain also labored at making the interior just as ornate. The living room's crowning detail was an elegant false fireplace built out of the bench from the wheelhouse of the Florence S.

Kitty lived in the house until her death in 1931. She was eccentric and also a hoarder, stashing money in cans and packages hidden around her house. According to a brochure published by the Pioneers of Alaska, Captain Smythe went through the house after her death hunting for valuables she might have squirreled away. A subsequent owner removed the false fireplace and found, among other items, a package of gold dust worth $350 at the time.

Her house was moved to its present location at Pioneer Park in 1967. It is now operated during the summer as a museum by the Pioneers of Alaska, Auxiliary No. 8.

Sources:

- Conversation with Joyce Wilson, Kitty Hensley House docent. 2011
- "Kitty and the Captain." Corrine Smith. *Fairbanks Daily News-Miner.* Dec. 15, 1996
- *Kitty Hensley House*. No author cited. Brochure produced by Pioneers of Alaska, Women's Auxiliary No. 8. 2010
- Letters and other records kept at Kitty Hensley House
- Yukon Riverboat Captains website. Jerry Green. Miami University. 2011

Fairbanks - Pioneer Park, Gold Rush Town

Gold Rush Town church originally graced downtown Fairbanks

First Presbyterian Church (now at Pioneer Park) in 1910

The picturesque wood-frame church at Pioneer Park is one of the oldest buildings in the park's gold rush town. However, the structure's front facade looks much different now than when it was the Presbyterian Church in downtown Fairbanks.

The Presbyterian Church grew interested in the Fairbanks area when rumors of gold discoveries began circulating in 1902. According to a history of First Presbyterian Church Fairbanks written by Charles Gray, during the winter of 1902-03 the Presbyterian missionary at Rampart (about 85 miles to the northeast on the Yukon River) hiked overland to check out the gold strike. Thinking the nascent town of Chena (at the confluence of the Chena and Tanana rivers) would be the area's main settlement, he built a mission cabin there and held the first church service in the Tanana Valley.

In July 1904, Reverend Howard Frank and wife took over the mission at Chena. Several weeks later Reverend S. Hall

Young, another Presbyterian missionary, stepped off the riverboat in Fairbanks to establish a church. Downtown lots were prohibitively expensive, so he bought a lot on the town's outskirts at the corner of Seventh Avenue and Cushman Street. The book, *Fairbanks, a City Historic Building Survey*, states that he raised construction funds through a public subscription from businesses and individuals, and had a small wood-frame church and cabin built for $5,500. A two-story manse replaced the cabin in 1908.

The Presbyterian Church faced Cushman Street and the front façade featured a central stained glass window, with a squat steeple and entrance on the left front corner of the building. The drawing shows the church in 1910 after a spire with belfry was added to the steeple. The manse is to the right of the church.

Within a few years Chena's fortunes were declining and Fairbanks was ascendant. The Chena mission was closed when Reverend Young left Fairbanks in 1906, and the Rev. Frank took over the Fairbanks church.

In 1931 a new larger sanctuary was built at the same site. The original church building was moved to the rear of the new sanctuary (facing Seventh Avenue), renamed Young Memorial Hall and used for Sunday school. It was then that the front façade was changed to resemble the present-day Pioneer Park church.

The steeple was removed, as well as the large stained glass window (which was installed in the new church). The front of the new Sunday school building received a central double-door, flanked by smaller stained glass windows, with a small circular window above the door.

By the mid 1950s the church had again outgrown its facility and the 1930s church was razed to make way for a new sanctuary. The original 1904 building survived however — still used for Sunday school. It wasn't until the mid-1960s that the church needed the space occupied by the old church building for a new Christian Education facility.

Fortunately, the A-67 site (now Pioneer Park) was being constructed to observe the 100th year celebration of Alaska's purchase from Russia, and the old church building was moved to its present site in the Gold Rush Town. Now the Pioneer Park church looks as if it has always been nestled next to Judge Wickersham's house (also built in 1904). It is open to the public and still used for church services and weddings.

Sources:

- *Fairbanks, a City Historic Building Survey*. Janet Matheson. City of Fairbanks. 1985
- "Fairbanks & the Presbyterian Church." Rev. H. Gene Straatmeyer. Presbytery of the Yukon website. 1979
- *History of First Presbyterian Church Fairbanks*. Charles Gray. Fairbanks. 1997
- Photo of Presbyterian church in 1910, from Charles E. Bunnell Collection. University of Alaska Fairbanks, Archives

Wickersham House in 2010

Judge Wickersham brought stability (and culture) to Fairbanks

Judge James Wickersham was not favorably impressed when he arrived in Fairbanks on April 9, 1903. The judge was traveling to Fairbanks from Circle City via dog sled, and in his book, *Old Yukon: Trails, Tales and Trials*, Wickersham said that as he and his dog team came out of the forest onto the north shore of the Chena River "... the new Metropolis of the Tanana River came into view on the opposite shore. A rough log structure, with spread-eagle wings, looked like a disreputable pig sty, but was in fact, Barnette's trading post, the only mercantile establishment in the new camp."

A hundred yards upriver sat a half-finished, two-story log building, without doors or windows, which announced itself as the Fairbanks Hotel. There were also two log cabins serving as saloons, a half-dozen smaller log cabin residences, and numerous tent frames. It was certainly not an auspicious introduction to the new home of the Third Judicial District.

Wickersham and his family had come north from Tacoma, Washington to Eagle, Alaska in 1900 when he was appointed judge to the newly formed Third Judicial District of the Territory of Alaska, a 300,000-square-mile area covering all of Interior and South-central Alaska.

Although based in Eagle, his duties took him wherever there were court cases. Those communities included Rampart, Circle City and Valdez. His schedule also allowed him to help with court cases in Alaska's other two judicial districts, and he spent considerable time in the Aleutians and in Nome.

While returning from Nome in 1902, Wickersham met E. T. Barnette at St. Michael. Wickersham was impressed with Barnette and suggested that he name his trading post after Senator Charles W. Fairbanks of Indiana (a friend and mentor of Wickersham). The judge said that if Barnette did so, he would do everything in his power to help the trader succeed.

Barnette subsequently changed his camp's name to Fairbanks, and Wickersham transferred his court's headquarters to the new boom town along the Chena. It should be said, however, that the move was based at least in part on Eagle's diminished population (and the reduced case load of the court there) as the Klondike Gold Rush ended and miners were lured to strikes elsewhere.

So Wickersham found himself in Fairbanks in 1903. Even though there was little in the way of amenities to recommend the town, Wickersham saw its possibilities and set to work, quickly appointing a justice of the peace and making plans for a courthouse and jail. (The courthouse would not be built until the next year)

Clara Rust's book, *Wickersham: the Man at Home*, records that the judge purchased a lot at the corner of First Avenue and Noble Street in April of 1904. With the help of a carpenter and day laborer, he began building a small, two-room cottage, the first frame house in the Tanana Valley.

Lumber for the house was purchased at a nearby sawmill and packed on shoulders back to the construction site since no wagons were available. By the end of the month the house was completed except for doors and windows, which would arrive via the first steamboat. That spring the judge also constructed a picket fence around the house, similar to the one around the house today.

Over the next few years, Wickersham improved the house. In 1906 he added two rooms: a parlor (the central portion of the house) and a small northwest bedroom. The judge also installed a hot-air furnace. Early photographs of the house show it looking much as it does today.

On one of his trips to the Lower 48 he purchased a phonograph. Once he got back to Fairbanks with the carefully packed phonograph and scores of tubular records, he would occasionally serenade the neighborhood by cranking up the phonograph and sticking its bell out the living-room window of his home.

The house was moved to Pioneer Park (then the A-67 Centennial site) in 1967. It has been restored and in 1979 was listed on the National Register of Historic Places. Furnished as it might have been when the Wickershams lived there, Wickersham House is now a museum operated by the Tanana-Yukon Historical Society.

Sources:

- *Fairbanks, a City Historic Building Survey*. Janet Matheson. City of Fairbanks. 1985
- Photos of Wickersham house in early 1900s, from John Zug Album. University of Alaska Fairbanks, Archives
- *Old Yukon: Tales, Trails and Trials*. James Wickersham. Washington Law Book Company. 1938
- *Wickersham: The Man at Home*. JoAnne Wold. Tanana-Yukon Historical Society. 1981
- *Wickersham House Museum*. Tanana-Yukon Historical Society. 2011

Fairbanks - Pioneer Park, Main entrance

SS Nenana along the lower Yukon River in the 1940s

SS Nenana, the last steamboat to Fairbanks

The SS Nenana has been one of the premier attractions at Pioneer Park. According to the book, "Fairbanks, A City Historic Building Survey," it is the largest sternwheel steamboat built west of the Mississippi River. It is also perhaps the last historic wooden-hulled sternwheeler in the United States. Other historic sternwheelers survive, but most of them have steel hulls. The only other surviving wooden-hulled sternwheelers I know of are the Klondike, Keno, and Moyie in Canada.

With its 20-year career, the Nenana was one of the exceptions among Yukon River wooden-hulled sternwheelers. These boats, built to navigate swift, shallow rivers, had light flat-bottomed flexible hulls, and were not known for longevity. Between groundings, boiler explosions, being crushed by ice and other accidents, the average lifespan of such riverboats was under 10 years.

The Alaska Railroad (ARR) operated the Nenana primarily on the Lower Yukon River. Designed by marine architect W.C. Nickum, the boat was prefabricated in Seattle and shipped piecemeal to the town of Nenana, where Berg Shipbuilding assembled it. Launched in May 1933, it is 237-feet long, 42-feet wide, and fully loaded drew about 3.5-feet of water. Its gross displacement is about 1,100 tons — capable of carrying 300 tons of freight. The Nenana could push six barges on the Yukon River, but was limited to one on the winding Tanana.

The boat is a packet (designed to carry passengers and freight). Stacked above the hull are five decks: a cargo deck, "saloon" deck with accommodations for 48 passengers, boat deck, "Texas" deck with crew quarters; and the pilot house.

Charles Adams (of Lavelle Young fame) was her first captain. When Charles retired in 1942, his nephew, Howard Adams, became the Nenana's captain.

During World War II, Yukon River steamboats in both Alaska and Canada were pressed into military service. In Canada, American-Yukon Navigation Company boats supported construction of the Alcan Highway and CANOL pipeline. In Alaska, the SS Nenana and its siblings transported personnel and supplies to Galena's military air field and to numerous smaller military installations along the Lower Yukon.

After the war ended, the Nenana made 1,600-mile-long round-trips between Nenana (on the Tanana) and Marshall (on the Lower Yukon) every two weeks during the summer. Occasionally it travelled upriver to Fort Yukon.

The Nenana's last year of service with the ARR was 1953. Airplanes had stolen all her passengers, and more efficient freight carriers were replacing steamers.

Yutana Barge Line leased the Nenana in 1954 for a single season. In 1957 a group from Fairbanks purchased the boat and brought her up the Tanana and Chena rivers to her final home. Howard Adams was captain for the last voyage.

The railroad bridge at Nenana really sealed the fate of the Fairbanks waterfront, since the bridge's low deck prevented steamboats from passing underneath. The SS Nenana's stack had to be lowered to get under the bridge. Rick Nerland, whose father was one of the people responsible for bringing the boat to Fairbanks, told me that even then it only cleared the bottom of the bridge by six inches.

The Nenana experienced major changes and trauma after arriving. In preparation for Fairbanks' 1967 centennial celebration, most of the cargo deck equipment was removed, the saloon deck was converted to a restaurant, and the Texas deck converted to a meeting room. During the 1967 Fairbanks flood the boat's cargo deck was deliberately flooded so the boat wouldn't float away.

The Fairbanks Historic Preservation Foundation restored the boat in the late 1980s, and in 1989 it was designated a National Historic Landmark. Restoration work did not include replacing the cargo deck's equipment. Much of that space was eventually filled with interpretive displays.

Unfortunately, deferred maintenance undid much of the restoration work, and, according to *Fairbanks Daily News-Miner* articles, in 2018 the Nenana was declared unsafe and closed to the public. The newspaper also reported that the Fairbanks North Star Borough, which owns the Nenana, lacked the funds to repair it. It was possible that the Nenana might be demolished or only a portion of it saved.

A nonprofit organization, Friends of the SS Nenena, was formed, and residents rallied behind the riverboat's survival. Borough officials were pursuaded to look for ways to save the vessel, and current plans now call for beginning restoration work on the SS Nenana in 2023.

Sources:

- Correspondence with Rick Nerland, whose father, Jerry Nerland, was one of the people responsible for bringing the SS Nenana to Fairbanks.
- *Fairbanks, a City Historic Building Survey*. Janet Matheson. City of Fairbanks. 1985
- "Interior of riverboat SS Nenana closing to public because of structural concerns." Sam Friedman. In *Fairbanks Daily News-Miner*. 3-23-2018
- "Nenana" entry, in *H. W. McCurdy Marine History of the Pacific Northwest*. Gordon R. Newell. Superior Publishing Company. 1966
- "Steamboat Nenana National Register of Historic Places Registration Form." Kevin J. Foster & William S. Hanable. National Park Service. 1988
- *Yukon River Steamboats*. Stan Cohen. Pictorial Histories Publishing Company. 1982

Fairbanks - Pioneer Park, Railroad Museum

Tanana Valley Railroad Engine No. 1 in 1996

The Tanana Valley Railroad and Engine No. 1, the Gold Dust Line

When Falcon Joslin, the mastermind behind the Tanana Valley Railroad (TVRR), began work on the line in 1904, he envisioned a railroad stretching from Fairbanks to Nome. However, real-world considerations meant the completed railroad reached only 39 miles, as far as Chatanika.

According to Nicholas Deely's book, *Tanana Valley Railroad, The Gold Dust Line,* the TVRR (originally the Tanana Mines Railway) began at the townsite of Chena, near the confluence of the Tanana and Chena Rivers.

Little track was laid during the first year, but by July of 1905 the tracks reached Fairbanks, just in time for the arrival of the railroad's first locomotive. Engine No. 1, a small H. K. Porter locomotive (shown in the drawing), came from the Yukon Territory's Coal Creek Coal Company, which

Joslin helped build, and it had been the first locomotive in the Yukon Territory.

Construction on the TVRR continued during 1905 on the railbed to Fox and Gilmore, and by September 1905 this initial phase was completed. The second phase, extending the line to Chatanika, was finished in 1907.

Unfortunately, railroad revenues began declining in 1910, and by 1917 the TVRR was insolvent. The Alaska Engineering Commission (AEC - precursor to the Alaska Railroad) which was building a standard-gauge railroad (4 feet 8.5 inches between rails) north from Anchorage, acquired the narrow-gauge TVRR (3 feet between rails), and it became the AEC's Chatanika Branch.

The AEC built another narrow-gauge branch from Fairbanks to Nenana to meet the northbound track. When the railroad's Tanana River bridge was completed in 1923, this section was widened to standard-gauge as far as Happy (in Goldstream valley) where the TVRR's tracks turned east toward Fox. That same year the AEC became the Alaska Railroad.

From Happy to Fairbanks the railroad laid one additional rail parallel to the narrow-gauge rails. This created a dual-gauge railway, allowing narrow-gauge and standard-gauge trains to use the same railbed.

Faced with improved local roads and increasing competition from motor vehicles, the ARR was forced to shut down the Chatanika Branch in 1930. The branch's rolling stock was scrapped, relocated or converted to standard-gauge, and the track was torn up and salvaged.

The right-of-way is still visible in areas such as Fox Gulch. Please note that the railroad's right-of-way, which crosses both public and private lands, was vacated years ago. Check land status before hiking and respect private property.

Engine No. 1, retired in 1922 and donated to the city of Fairbanks, fortunately escaped destruction. It was long on display in front of the Fairbanks depot, and eventually moved to what is now called Pioneer Park.

A group of volunteers (including myself), formed the Friends of the Tanana Valley Railroad in 1991 to restore the engine.

There was much work in store for us. For example, the locomotive's water tank and wooden cab were in deplorable condition and had to be replaced. (Our carpenter and I actually traveled to Dawson City to take measurements, photos and sketches of the cab on No. 1's sister engine—No. 4.) We had also hoped to restore the boiler, but decided it was safer (albeit more expensive) to manufacture a replacement boiler utilizing some of the old boiler's parts.

The engine restoration was completed in 2000 and the little locomotive now chugs around the tracks at Pioneer Park on special occasions.

By the way, the last engine purchased for use on the Chatanika branch was a Baldwin 4-6-0 locomotive, brought into service by the AEC in 1920. It is also still in service—on the Huckleberry Railroad at historic Crossroads Village, near Flint, Michigan.

Sources:

- Conversations with Dan Gullickson, past president and founding member of Friends of the Tanana Valley Railroad
- Dawson City Railroad Museum, Dawson City, Yukon Territory, Canada
- *Historic Resources in the Fairbanks North Star Borough.* Janet Matheson & F. Bruce Haldeman. Fairbanks North Star Borough. 1981
- *Tanana Valley Railroad, the Gold Dust Line.* Nicholas Deely. Denali Designs. 1996
- "The History of the Tanana Valley Railroad." No author cited. Friends of the Tanana Valley Railroad website. 2011
- "The Little Engine that did." Mary Fenno. *Fairbanks Daily News-Miner.* August 17, 1997

South Fairbanks - Peger Road

ARC grader at Alaska DOT in 2002

The Alaska Road Commission, 55 years helping develop Alaska

An old horse-drawn grader (shown in the drawing) sits at the Alaska Department of Transportation offices on Peger Road in Fairbanks, just down the street from Pioneer Park. Built by Western Wheeled Scraper in Aurora, Illinois, it is probably one of the earliest graders still in existence in Alaska, dating from about 1900. (The design was patented in 1892.) It's an amazing machine, and incorporates most of the movements standard on modern motorized graders. Of course, all the controls on the grader were operated by hand and it must have taken a burly operator.

It was utilized by the Alaska Road Commission (ARC), the entity responsible for trail and road construction throughout Alaska from 1905 to 1960. Prior to the ARC's creation, the federal government, through several laws, had tried building roads in the territory.

According to the book, *Blazing Alaska's Trails,* the federal government passed a law in 1898 authorizing the construction of toll roads and bridges in Alaska, but few took advantage of the law. Those that did often had trouble collecting the tolls. Congress tried again with a 1904 law that set up road districts with local road overseers, and required every able-bodied Alaskan male living outside incorporated towns to provide two days labor or eight dollars cash each year for road and trail construction. Only a few local roads and trails (often of poor quality) were constructed under this act.

These attempts proved inadequate in part because the government did not take an active role or provide direct funding. The Nelson Act of 1905 changed that. Claus-M. Naske's book, *Paving Alaska's Trails - the work of the Alaska Road Commission*, relates that the act established a "Board of Road Commissioners for Alaska" (more commonly called the Alaska Road Commission). The ARC, under War Department authority, was tasked with constructing and maintaining trails and roads in the territory, and was overseen (at least in its early years) by a board of three Army officers. Its first chairman was Brigadier General Wilds P. Richardson. The commission was funded through a combination of fees and direct appropriations from Congress.

The ARC began work immediately—flagging winter trails, upgrading and blazing new trails, and constructing roads. The early years were arduous, with the ARC having to deal with permafrost, rugged terrain, and seasonally swollen streams. In permafrost areas, corduroy roads were constructed (logs were laid perpendicular to the roadway and covered by gravel). Bridge building was avoided by fording small streams and using ferries to cross major rivers (such as the Tanana at Big Delta). One of its earliest projects was upgrading the Fairbanks-Valdez trail to a wagon road (completed by 1910).

In 1932 the ARC was transferred to the Department of the Interior. By that time it had constructed over 1,000 miles of roads, and over 4,000 miles of trails.

The Bureau of Public Roads, which eventually became the Federal Highway Administration, assumed responsibility for the ARC in 1956--an important milestone since it could now receive federal funds under the Federal Aid Highway Act. In 1960 the ARC was transferred to the new State of Alaska, becoming the Alaska Department of Highways.

Many of Alaska's historic highways are named for Road Commission officers instrumental in their construction: the Richardson for Brigadier General Wilds Richardson, the Steese for Colonel James Steese, the Elliott for Major Malcolm Elliott, the Edgerton for Major General Glen Edgerton, and the Taylor for ARC president Ike Taylor.

When the State assumed the ARC's responsibilities, it took over the maintenance of about 3,000 miles of roads, most constructed by the commission.

Although the ARC is gone, its equipment and buildings can still be seen at places such as Big Delta State Historical Park, The Alaska Department of Trasnportation offices in Fairbanks, or scattered along roadsides across the state.

Sources:

- *Alaska Road Commission Historical Narrative – Final Report.* Claus-M. Naske. State of Alaska. 1983
- *Alaska's Heritage, Chapter4-10: Road Construction.* Alaska Humanities Forum. The Alaska History & Cultural Studies Website. 2004
- *Blazing Alaska's Trails.* Alfred Hulse Brooks. University of Alaska & Arctic Institute of North America. 1953
- *Giant Earthmovers.* Keith Haddock. Motorbooks International. 1998
- *Paving Alaska's Trails - the work of the Alaska Road Commission.* Claus-M. Naske. University Press of America. 1986

Ben Eielson's Curtis Wright JN-4 (Jenny) as it looked in the 1920s

Ben Eielson and his Jenny fly into Alaska history

Carl Ben Eielson, one of Alaska's pioneering aviators, grew up yearning to fly. Born in North Dakota in 1897, he got his chance to become a pilot during World War I by enlisting in the U.S. Army. Eielson completed flight training and received orders to sail for France, but the war ended before he shipped out. He was discharged in March 1919.

Eielson spent the next several years alternating between barnstorming and attending college. While studying at Georgetown Law School (now Georgetown University) in Washington, D.C., he met Daniel Sutherland, Alaska's delegate to Congress, who persuaded Eielson to teach in Alaska.

In 1922, Eielson arrived in Fairbanks to teach secondary school. Teaching couldn't prevent him from dreaming about flying, however, and he soon convinced several Fairbanks businessmen to back him in forming the Farthest North Airplane Company.

He bought a U.S. Army surplus Curtiss Wright JN-4D (a Jenny) and was soon ferrying supplies, mail and passengers between communities and mining camps.

In February 1924, he flew Alaska's first air-mail run, from Fairbanks to McGrath. Eielson took about four hours to cover that distance, which would have taken two weeks by Alaska's normal winter mail delivery system—sled dog.

Eielson went on to achieve many other aviation firsts. He teamed up with Australian explorer Hubert Wilkins for several Arctic expeditions. In 1927, they made the first known landing on pack ice. The next year (1928) Eielson and Hubert flew from Alaska to Greenland, the first flight over the North Pole. Later that year they also flew over Antarctica, becoming the first men to fly over both polar regions in the same year.

Two years later Eielson was killed in a plane accident. In November 1929, he and his mechanic, Earl Borland, crashed while flying a Hamilton airplane to evacuate passengers and cargo from a stranded ship off the coast of Siberia. It took search parties over two months to find the crash site.

Fortunately for aviation history, the owners of the first plane that Eielson used in Alaska (the Curtiss Wright Jenny) donated it to the University of Alaska. The plane was disassembled and stored at the university for many years.

Eventually, the plane was reassembled and displayed at the Fairbanks International Airport passenger terminal. However, the wings it wore were not its own. Evidently, the plane was moved to Eielson Air Force base for reassembly and while there, its wings were accidentally destroyed. The ever-resourceful airplane assemblers replaced the missing wings with those from another plane in the university collection, a Swallow biplane.

That was how things stood until new construction at the airport passenger terminal meant the Jenny needed to be moved. Volunteers from the Farthest North Chapter of the Experimental Aircraft Association (Chapter 1129) stepped forward to make things right. In 2007, they began the time-consuming process of finding original plans and fabricating new wings.

Roger Weggel, coordinator of the restoration project, told me that during their research they discovered what a rare bird Eielson's Jenny is. While a few score Jennies still exist (even several that fly), most of those other planes have been extensively rebuilt. Except for the new wings and the engine, everything else about Eielson's plane is original. (Eielson replaced the original Curtis OX-5 engine with a Hispano-Suiza engine — standard in the later JN-4H).

While work on the wings proceeded, the rest of the plane was disassembled and refinished. After the wings were completed in 2012 the plane was carefully re-assembled. In October of 2013 Eielson's Jenny was re-installed at the Fairbanks airport passenger terminal, suspended over the main luggage carousel.

Sources:

- "Carl 'Ben' Eielson," in Farthest North Collegian. University of Alaska. June 30, 1930
- Conversation with Roger Weggel, instructor in UAF Aviation Technology Program
- *Brother to the Eagle, the Story of Carl Ben Eielson.* Erling Nicolai Rolfsrud. Lantern Books. 1952
- *Polar Pilot, the Carl Ben Eielson Story.* Dorothy Page. Hobart Pbns. 1992
- *The Complete Encyclopedia of World Aircraft.* David Donald, editor. Barnes & Noble. 1997

Fairbanks - Garden Island, N. Turner Street

Northern Commercial Company warehouses in 2008

Warehouse all that's left of Fairbanks Northern Commercial Company

The accompanying drawing shows two warehouses on the north bank of the Chena River that were once owned by the Northern Commercial Company. NC Company was a powerhouse of Alaska commerce during the late 1800s and early 1900s, owning stores throughout Alaska and the Yukon. Its sister business, Northern Navigation Company, operated scores of steamboats.

Company officials were always scouting for new mercantile opportunities, acquiring existing trading posts or opening new stores. When NC Company representatives investigated the Tanana Valley diggings in February of 1903, E. T. Barnette (owner of Barnette's Cache) saw either the writing on the wall... or a golden opportunity. He quickly departed for The NC Company headquarters in San Francisco to negotiate with company officials for the sale of his trading post.

According to the book, *Crooked Past, the History of a Frontier Mining Camp,* the NC Company agreed to purchase a two-thirds share in Barnette's trading post. The company soon began expanding the trading post's operation, and the next year bought out Barnette entirely. By 1905 the company's Fairbanks facilities covered two city blocks on the south bank of the Chena River. Facilities included an enlarged store, offices, machine shop, power plant, dock, and six warehouses.

The book, *Fairbanks, a City Historic Building Survey,* relates that The Dominion Commercial Company built two warehouses across the river from the N C Company in 1905, and several years later NC acquired those warehouses for its burgeoning Fairbanks operation. Today, only one warehouse remains on the north bank (the center one in the drawing). It is the oldest industrial building in Fairbanks and last visible sign of the NC Company's presence in town.

The Chena River's channel was wider in the early 1900s, and the warehouses were originally mere yards from the river bank. Extensive landfill in front of the warehouses pushed the river's edge several hundred feet away. The buildings have post and beam wood framing with 2x wood flooring and corrugated metal sheathing covering walls and roof. (Corrugated metal sheathing was the de rigueur standard for building facades in early Fairbanks.) New layers of metal sheathing were eventually lapped over the old.

The buildings, because of their proximity to the river and almost annual flooding, were constructed on pilings. Over the years there has been differential settling of the pilings and the warehouse floor now rolls like an uneasy ocean. There is a difference of almost a foot in elevation between parts of the floor.

Construction of the new Barnette Street bridge has forced some unwanted changes. Samson Hardware's two-story warehouse immediately east of the NC warehouses (in the drawing background) has been demolished, along with Samson Hardware's Illinois Street store.

John Jackovich, owner of the remaining NC Company warehouse, also owns the Big I Pub next door. The pub's parking lot was lost to the roadway leading to the new bridge, so Jackovich was forced to demolish the smaller warehouse (to the left in the drawing) and part of the larger one to put in a new parking lot. However, he appears determined to preserve at least a part of the NC Company's heritage — keeping the remaining warehouse and gradually fixing it up.

It seems a few more old Fairbanks buildings disappear every year. I hope this warehouse will be around for a while longer and that residents don't forget the vital role the NC Company played in building Fairbanks.

Sources:

- Conversation with John Jackovich, current owner of warehouse
- *Crooked Past, The History of a Frontier Mining Camp: Fairbanks, Alaska.* Terrence Cole. University of Alaska Press. 1991,
- *Fairbanks, a City Historic Building Survey.* Janet Matheson. City of Fairbanks. 1985
- *Flag over the North, the Story of the Northern Commercial Company.* Lois Delano Kitchener. Superior Publishing Company. 1954
- *Tracing the Assets of the Russian-American Company, 1867-1943.* Steve Lloyd. 2003

Fairbanks - Garden Island, N Cushman Street

Immaculate Conception Church in 2011

Immaculate Conception Church a moving experience

Some buildings, because of location or design, are picturesque from the moment they are completed. Others acquire character as they settle into the landscape. Immaculate Conception Church has had its charm bequeathed to it by time and the efforts of its priests and parishioners.

When the church was constructed during the fall and winter of 1904-05, it was an unimposing single-story wood-frame structure at the corner of First Avenue and Dunkel Street (on the south side of the Chena River just a few blocks from the riverfront). According to the book, *Fairbanks, a City Historic Building Survey*, there was little to distinguish it as a church.

One of the few things that did set the building apart was its size (65 feet by 30 feet). An article celebrating the church's 2004 centennial appeared in the Catholic newsletter, *The Alaska Shepherd*. It mentioned that Father Francis Monroe, the priest responsible for its construction, was chastised by some townsfolk for building such a large church since, "There would never be enough Catholics in Fairbanks to justify the size."

Father Monroe found himself busy though, especially after the Catholic Church built St. Joseph's Hospital on the north side of the river in 1906. (The hospital closed in the late 1960s and was later torn down. Denali State Bank now occupies St. Joseph's three-story concrete addition that was constructed in the 1950s.)

The hospital and church were on opposite banks of the river, and Father Monroe quickly faced a quandary. As church and hospital-related duties increased, he found himself spending more and more time commuting. What to do? Build a new church near the hospital? No, he decided, move the existing structure across the river.

Many thought the priest's plan to move the church building was folly, but Monroe was undaunted. The Catholics acquired the lot next to the hospital, (originally the site of a sawmill), excavated for a basement and put in a foundation. In the fall of 1911 the church building was hauled by horse-team the few blocks to the river. Then everyone waited for freeze-up.

In November, when the river ice was thick enough to support a horse team, parallel lines (about 30 feet apart) were laid out diagonally across the river and holes chipped through the ice 8 feet apart along the lines. Pilings were inserted through the holes, driven into the river bottom, allowed to freeze in place and cut off several feet above the ice. Heavy timbers laid over the pilings thus formed rough trestles across the river. The church building could then be pulled across the river on logs spanning the trestles.

It was quite a day's entertainment when the building finally inched across the trestles. Apparently, betting was brisk on whether the move would be successful. (Odds did not favor it.) But there were no major problems and the building was hauled up a rough roadway cut into the opposite bank and into position on the foundation. In the spring of 1912, the basement was completed and a two-story attached residence was added.

In 1914, the church's ceiling was raised, a more steeply-pitched roof was constructed and the narthex (entry) and belfry (bell tower) were added. The additional five feet in ceiling height allowed a choir loft to be built. It was then that the larger-than-life statue of "Our Lady of the Immaculate Conception" was placed on the narthex roof.

The church's stained glass windows were installed in 1926. Sometime later, the sanctuary's walls and ceiling were finished with carved wood wainscoting, wood molding, and high-ornamented pressed-tin panels.

Immaculate Conception Church was listed on the National Register of Historic Places in 1976 and is now one of the most-photographed landmarks in Fairbanks.

Sources:

- "Immaculate Conception Parish in Fairbanks celebrates a century of faith: 1904-2004," in *The Alaska Shepard*. Father Louis L. Renner & Patty Walter. Catholic Bishops of Northern Alaska. Fairbanks. August/September 2004,
- "Immaculate Conception Church History." No author. ICC web page. 2011
- *Fairbanks, a City Historic Building Survey*. Janet Matheson. City of Fairbanks. 1985,
- *Buildings of Alaska*. Alison K. Hoagland. Oxford University Press. 1993
- Photos of Immaculate Conception Church at Dunkel Street location, from Charles E. Bunnell Collection. University of Alaska Fairbanks, Archives
- Photo of Immaculate Conception Church at present location in 1937, from Woodrow Johansen Papers. University of Alaska Fairbanks, Archives

Fairbanks - Garden Island, Driveway Street

West Coast Grocery warehouse in 2011

West Coast Grocery warehouse and a ghost of Christmas past

The unpretentious metal-sided building at 318 Driveway Street (across from the News-Miner building) looks similar to the Northern Commercial Company (NC Company) warehouse at the end of Turner Street (a few blocks away, near the river). Since it began life as a warehouse for the West Coast Grocery, any similarity in design and construction is understandable.

Built in 1936, (about 30 years younger than the NC Company building) the grocery warehouse is elevated above the ground on a post and pad foundation, just as the NC warehouse is elevated on pilings. In addition, both buildings are of post and beam construction (also called timber framing) and sheathed with corrugated metal siding and roofing.

West Coast Grocery, a wholesaler serving small grocery stores such as Lindy's, closed in the mid 1960s. The building has seen several owners since then, but is now owned by Johnson River Enterprises, run by Sonny Lindner (the Yukon Quest and Iditarod musher).

During renovations, much of the interior has been remodeled, but a December 10, 2010 article in the *Fairbanks Daily News-Miner* says Lindner, who is interested in historic preservation, decided not to replace the corrugated metal siding. Consequently, the building's exterior still looks similar to the way it did years ago. (You can still see lettering from West Coast Grocery days on the northeast facade.)

Lindner also faced foundation problems. Although differential settling had caused rippling of the floor he decided the best course of action was to just stabilize rather than replace the post and pad foundation.

Since the building used to be a grocery warehouse, I thought I could talk about a "cold-storage Christmas" and what Christmas dinner used to be like back in the "good old days." Imagine my disappointment when a friend and long-time Fairbanks resident, Glenn Gibson, said Christmas dinner during the 50s and 60s wasn't much different from now.

It's true that in the early 1900s the bulk of Fairbanks freight had to come via ship (usually an Alaska Steamship Company vessel) to St. Michael's (on Norton Sound near the mouth of the Yukon River), and by riverboats up the Yukon and Tanana rivers. Small amounts also came by ship to Valdez and then overland along the Valdez-Alaska Trail. The only "fresh" foods available during much of the year were those grown and stored locally. Completion of the Alaska Railroad in 1923 improved this somewhat but freight still had to come by steamer from Seattle to Seward.

The advent of air travel changed all that. Pan American World Airways (through its Alaska subsidiary, Pacific Alaska Airways) began flights from Juneau to Fairbanks in 1932. The airlines received permission in 1940 to fly directly from Seattle to Alaska, and by the 50s the airline was flying two or three times a week into Fairbanks. During that time period it used Douglas DC-6s, which (depending on configuration) could carry up to 28,188 pounds of freight, or up to 102 passengers. (These were the same type of aircraft Pan Am used on its first trans-Atlantic tourist class flights, starting in 1952.)

With fresh groceries arriving on regular flights, Fairbanks residents achieved a rough parity with their cousins in the lower 48 (at least in availability if not price). Of course, that parity didn't extend to communities not linked to Fairbanks by road or rail.

Sources:

- "Alaska Construction Company Revitalizes Historic Fairbanks Warehouse." Reba Lean. *Fairbanks Daily News-Miner*. December 11, 2010
- *Alaska's Heritage,* Chapter 4-12 Air Transportation. The Alaska History & Cultural Studies Website. Alaska Humanities Forum. 2004
- Conversation with Glenn Gibson, long-time Fairbanks resident "DC-6/C-118A Liftmaster Transport History." Boing International website. 2012
- *Fairbanks, a City Historic Building Survey*. Janet Matheson. City of Fairbanks. 1985
- Fairbanks North Star Borough land records
- Photos of DC-6 in Fairbanks, from Captain Ralph W. Savory Collection (Savory was the chief pilot for the Alaska region of Pan American World Airways). University of Alaska Fairbanks, Archives

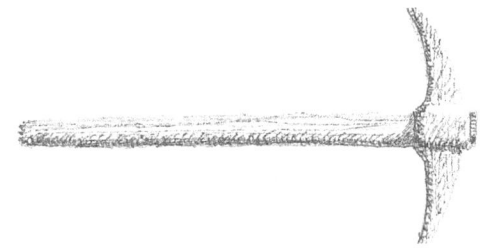

Fairbanks - Phillips Field Road

Fairbanks coal bunkers in 1995

Fairbanks coal bunkers were the last of their kind in Alaska

Fairbanks was never a coal-mining town, but coal did help Fairbanks recover from the lean times of the late 1910s and early 1920s. In 1910 about 11,000 people lived in the Fairbanks area (the city had 3,541 residents) but after the drift mines were played out, most miners moved on. By 1920 the city had shrunk to about 1,100 residents and most mining camps were virtually deserted.

The opening of the Alaska Agricultural College and School of Mines in 1922 began to revive Fairbanks. However, John Boswell, in his book on the history of the Fairbanks Exploration Company (FE Company), shows that the company's gold dredges (which began operating in the late 1920s) were what really returned prosperity to the area. And the FE Company's operations would not have been possible without the completion of the Alaska Railroad in 1923, coupled with the nearby and readily accessible coal mines at Suntrana (present-day Healy area).

Coal provided power for the dredges, but also found a ready market elsewhere in Fairbanks. Nearby hills had been denuded of trees to provide timbers for mines, lumber for construction, and cordwood to fire boilers and heat buildings. People readily converted to coal since wood was becoming scarce.

In 1932 the Fairbanks coal bunkers (shown in the drawing) were built at 270 Illinois Street by the Healy River Coal Corporation. Of heavy timber-frame construction, the bunkers were 54 feet tall and over 180 feet long.

Originally, a long inclined wooden railroad trestle led up to the bunkers and a locomotive would push loaded coal cars up the rails to dump their loads inside the top shed. Storage bins were located beneath the top floor and there were 13 chutes on either side of the structure for dispensing coal.

In the early 1960s the trestle was replaced by a steel conveyor system. With that system, coal was dumped into a pit about 70 feet from the bunkers, and the conveyor lifted the coal to the bunkers' top level. There it was transferred to a horizontal conveyor and dropped into storage bins.

Oil gradually replaced coal as the fuel of choice for most individuals and businesses, and by the 1990s the bunkers were selling little coal. The owners of OK Lumber (their store was beside the bunkers) bought the structure in 1996, planning to dismantle it to expand their store operation. In December of that year the last load of coal was sold.

Hearing of the plans to dismantle the bunkers, the "Friends of the Coal Bunkers" organized in an effort to save the structure. Randy Griffin (one of the group's organizers) told me that unfortunately, even with the support of many Fairbanks residents, the group was unable to secure a place to move the bunkers to, or the funds necessary to save even a small portion of it. Eventually, most of the timbers were salvaged and used for other construction projects.

A small section of the bunkers was donated to the owners of Gold Dredge No. 8 and now sits on its side at the gold dredge parking lot in Fox. Other bit and pieces of the bunkers, like the ventilators that used to sit atop the roof, are lying in people's back yards.

Bunkers also used to be located in Anchorage, Cordova, Nenana and Skagway, but those disappeared years ago. The Fairbanks coal bunkers were the last of their kind in Alaska.

Sources:

- *Chronicle of Alaska Coal-Mining History.* Roy D. Merritt. Alaska Division of Geological and Geophysical Surveys. 1986
- Conversation with Randy Griffin, one of the organizers of "Friends of the Coal Bunkers"
- *Fairbanks, a City Historic Building Survey.* Janet Matheson. City of Fairbanks. 1985
- *Fairbanks, A Pictorial History.* Claus-M. Naske & Ludwig Rowinski. The Donning Company Publishers. 1981
- Photos of coal bunkers, from Charles E. Bunnell Collection. University of Alaska Fairbanks. Archives
- The Fairbanks Coal Bunkers website. Randy Griffin webmaster. 1998

Fairbanks - Illinois Street

FE Company office building in 1991

Fairbanks Exploration Company revived early Fairbanks

This drawing depicts the Fairbanks Exploration Company (FE Company) office building as it looked in 1991. Janet Matheson's book, *Fairbanks, a City Historic Building Survey*, records that this stately building, constructed in 1926, was the first concrete block building in Fairbanks. Locally manufactured concrete blocks, fashioned to mimic natural stone, were used in its construction.

Behind the office building is the gold recovery room where amalgam (an alloy of gold and mercury) was processed, and across the railroad tracks in the background is the company's two-story machine shop.

The FE Company was a subsidiary of U.S. Smelting, Refining and Mining Company (a 1916 *New York Times* article described the USSR&MC as the second largest smelting company in the US.) It became interested in Fairbanks in the early 1920s, when the city's fortunes were at low ebb. Gold production, as well as the area's population, had been steadily declining for over a decade. The city's population dropped from a high of 6000 residents in 1905 to 1400 people in 1920.

The problem was that most of the gold around Fairbanks lay entombed under tens if not hundreds of feet of frozen overburden. Because of the cost in time, labor, equipment and supplies, during the area's early years it was only profitable to mine the richest and most easily accessible placers. As the easy diggings disappeared it became harder to mine profitably.

In the early 1920s several developments brought Fairbanks back to prosperity. The Alaska Railroad (from Seward to Fairbanks) was completed in 1923, providing inexpensive and dependable transportation. Heavy equipment, like gold dredges (which could take advantage of low-grade gold placers), could then be brought in. Also, the opening of the Suntrana and Healy coal fields provided cheap and plentiful fuel. Large corporations, with the deep pockets necessary to bring in heavy equipment and develop the gold fields were now interested in Fairbanks.

The FE Company was but one of several companies that began dredging in the Fairbanks area, but it was the most successful. It began acquiring individual claims in 1924, consolidating them into large blocks that could be efficiently mined using dredges. According to John Boswell's history of FE Company operations, three of its dredges began working in 1928, and by 1940 the company had eight dredges operating. Consequently, by 1940 the population of Fairbanks had rebounded to over 4,000 residents.

All FE Company dredges were idled during World War II, but by the 1950s seven were once again operating. The company began closing down dredging activities in 1958 and by 1963 its last dredge in the Fairbanks area was shut down. The FE Company sold off its remaining facilities and land in the 1990s.

According to the National Register of Historic Places, at the height of its activities the FE Company facilities on Illinois Street included the office building, gold recovery room, power plant, several shops and warehouses, and numerous houses built for employees. Most of the industrial buildings are gone. Only the office building and machine shop are left on the west side of Illinois. These two buildings, along with the employee housing on the east side of the street, form the Illinois Street Historic District. Six of the buildings: the machine shop, manager's house, and four employee houses, are listed on the National Register of Historic Places.

Golden Valley Electric Association now owns the old office building. In 2011 it completed an addition to the rear of the building that blends nicely with the original structure. The electric cooperative used to buy power from the FE Company and purchased the FE power plant in 1952. (It was retired in 1972.) I think it is fitting that GVEA now owns the building and is striving to preserve it.

Sources:

- Conversation with Pete Eagan, former manager of FE Company properties in Fairbanks area
- "Copper Stock Listed: United States Smelting, Refining & Mining Co. goes on Exchange." New York Times. March 23, 1916.
- *Fairbanks, a City Historic Building Survey.* Janet Matheson. City of Fairbanks. 1985
- Fairbanks North Star Borough property records
- *History of Alaskan Operations of United States Smelting, Refining and Mining Company.* John C. Boswell. Mineral Industry Research Laboratory, University of Alaska, Fairbanks. 1979
- "Illinois Street Historic District, National Register of Historic Places Registration Form." Judith Bittner. National Park Service, 2001

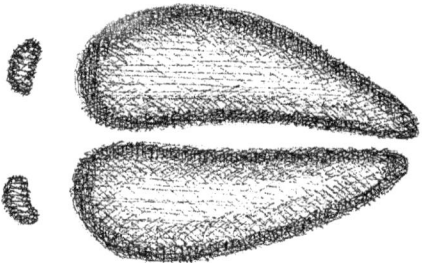

Fairbanks - Illinois Street

The "White House" in 1993

Remainder of Fairbanks Exploration Company housing lines Illinois Street

For more than 30 years, the Fairbanks Exploration Company (FE Company) maintained a company enclave at the north end of Illinois Street. The west side of the street is where the company's office and industrial facilities were located, and company housing lined the east side of the street.

The company or its employees once owned houses from Noyes Slough to Slater Street (kitty-corner to Phillips Field Road). At least 11 company houses used to stand there, but now only eight survive. All of these houses, as well as the office building and machine shop across the street, are included in the Illinois Street Historic District, established in 2001.

At the north end, on the bank of Noyes Slough, sits the grandest of the surviving FE Company houses, built for its general manager in 1935. Shown in the drawing, this was known as the "White House." It is a 3,746 square-foot two-and-a-half story Colonial Revival house set back from Illinois Street in a stand of trees.

Typical of Colonial Revival homes, it has a centrally-placed elaborate entry, with paired windows spaced symmetrically on either side. There is a large exterior brick chimney on the house's northeast side (facing Noyes Slough). The company power plant across the street supplied the house with steam heat.

The National Register of Historic Places registration form for the Historic District states that the "White House," along with a large tract of land, was sold to the Catholic Church in 1964 for the site of Monroe Catholic School. The house was the convent for nuns working at Monroe School until 1994, when it was sold to a private individual who has maintained it in near original condition.

To the south, on the far side of Monroe, is an FE Company housing complex now privately owned and called Tanana Mill Office Park. (Tanana Mill refers to the old sawmill that sat on the bank of Noyes Slough, about where the GVEA facilities are now.) This small planned community, constructed in 1927, consists of four similar bungalow-styled one-story houses with hipped tin roofs. Each house had its own greenhouse, with steam heat provided to the houses and greenhouses from the company power plant.

Of the surviving company houses, the oldest is the Noyes house at the corner of Illinois and Minnie Streets. Built in about 1911 by Fred Noyes (who owned the Tanana Mill lumber yard), the house was purchased by the FE Company in 1925 and used to house company employees. In 1959 it was sold to a local businessman and is now part of the Chapel of Chimes property. The building's exterior still retains many of its original features and details.

At the southern end of Illinois Street (on the far side of Minnie Street) are additional houses that, while not owned by the FE Company, were constructed by company employees in the early 1930s. There used to be four similarly styled houses between Minnie and Slater Street, but two were eliminated (one moved to Hamilton Acres subdivision) to make room for the Chevron service station at the corner of Minnie and Illinois Streets, across from the Noyes house. The two remaining structures are both Tudor Revival houses, typified by steeply pitched intersecting rooflines, paired windows, and decorative entryways.

The construction of Period Revival houses by the FE Company and its employees was part of a trend. According to the book, *Fairbanks, a City Historic Building Survey*, the building of these types of houses was, "a sign of community prosperity in the 1920s heralded by the arrival of the Alaska Railroad, the rise of air transportation, and the arrival of the FE Company."

Sources:

- *American Architecture since 1789.* Marcus Whiffen. Massachusetts Institute of Technology. 1969
- *Fairbanks, a City Historic Building Survey.* Janet Matheson. City of Fairbanks. 1985
- Fairbanks North Star Borough property records
- *History of Alaskan Operations of United States Smelting, Refining and Mining Company.* John C. Boswell. Mineral Industry Research Laboratory, University of Alaska, Fairbanks. 1979
- "Illinois Street Historic District, National Register of Historic Places Registration Form." Judith Bittner. National Park Service, 2001

Fairbanks - College Road, Fountainhead Antique Auto Museum

Fordson snow tractor in 2014 outside the Fountainhead Antique Auto Museum in Fairbanks

Fordson snow tractor and the Detroit-Arctic Expedition

The odd-looking contraption in the drawing is a Fordson "Snow Motor," also called a snow tractor. It is basically a Fordson tractor (built by the Ford Motor Company) with the wheels removed, and two large torpedo-shaped screws attached. The screws, which were counter-rotating and controlled by separate clutches, propelled the tractor across snow and ice.

The screws and related equipment were sold as a kit by the Armstead Snow Motor Company. A demonstration film made in the 1920s shows the vehicle to be speedy (for a tractor) and remarkably agile over snow-covered ice and deep pack snow. In the film the vehicle performed well on relatively level terrain, and was touted as being able to pull up to 20 tons. It seemed like just the vehicle for winter use in Alaska, but the first known attempt to use them in Interior Alaska resulted in failure.

In 1926 Australian aviator and explorer, George Hubert Wilkins, undertook an expedition to find a rumored large island, Keenan Land, in the middle of the Arctic Ocean. Arctic explorers for decades had been tantalized by sightings (what we now know to be mirages) of mountains to the north, across the Arctic Ocean. By foot, dogsled and boat they had been unable to come close to the island's supposed location, hundreds of miles north of Alaska. Wilkins proposed to use airplanes to explore the region instead.

Simon Nasht, in his book, *The Last Explorer: Hubert Wilkins, hero of the great age of polar exploration,* writes that Wilkins wanted to reach the "Pole of Inaccessibility," that point "furthest from all land masses and about 400 miles south of the North Pole." In that area Wilkins though Keenan Land, if it existed, must be.

With backing from the North American Newspaper Alliance and the Detroit Aviation Society, Wilkins organized the "Detroit Arctic Expedition," and hired Alaska aviator, Ben Eielson, as pilot.

Fairbanks, at the northern end of the Alaska Railroad, was the starting point for ferrying the expedition's two airplanes to Barrow, from whence flights out over the Arctic Ocean would originate.

However, Nenana, 60 miles to the south, was to be the jumping off point for an overland caravan hauling aviation fuel, radio equipment and other supplies for the expedition. Plans were to travel downriver to the village of Tanana, near the confluence of the Yukon and Tanana Rivers, and then strike out cross-country to Barrow.

To expedition organizers the Fordson snow tractors seemed an ideal choice for the Arctic caravan (with the addition of enclosed cabs), and three tractors were shipped to Nenana and assembled. Two tractors, each pulling five specially-designed cargo trailers, set out on February 10, 1926.

Unfortunately, they did not get far before encountering problems. After 12 days the snow tractors had only covered 65 miles.

According to a 1990 *Fairbanks Daily News-Miner* article, the tractor screws could not get adequate traction in Interior Alaska's dry powder snow, and their engines were troublesome in the region's frigid sub-zero temperatures.

I also noticed in the demonstration film that while the tractors worked well on relatively level ground, they had some trouble going over obstructions or rough ground.

Of course, there was also the seven-foot width of the snow tractor. The Alaska Road Commission typically blazed trails to a five-foot width. If the caravan left the river it would have encountered problems on most of the regions winter trails.

Also, the snow tractors had voracious appetites and would have burned through all the tractor and aviation fuel before reaching Barrow. Wilkins abandoned the snow tractors at Tolovana and flew gas for the airplanes to Barrow instead. The rest of the supplies reached Barrow via five dogsleds - a trip that took seven weeks.

What happened to the snow tractors next is a mystery, but one of them ended up in the possession of Fairbanks resident George Clayton. That machine was eventually acquired by the Pioneer Air Museum at Pioneer Park. It sat for years in front of the aviation museum and now is on loan to the Fountainhead Antique Auto Museum, which has restored the tractor to operating condition.

Sources:

- Demonstration film of Fordson Snow Motor, at "The Old Motor," an online vintage automobile magazine. <http://theoldmotor.com/>
- "Early snow tractors fail course on '26 trek." Eric Troyer. In *Fairbanks Daily News-Miner*. 4-1-1990
- *The Last Explorer: Hubert Wilkins, hero of the great age of polar exploration.* Simon Nasht. Arcade Publishing. 2005
- Signage at Fountainhead Antique Auto Museum
- "Wilkins-Eielson expeditions helped open arctic skies." Paul Solka. In *Fairbanks Daily News-Miner*. 4-1-1990

Fairbanks - College Road, Creamers Field

Creamer's Dairy in 1995. Tractor in drawing is the Farmall A sitting in one of the Dairy's equipment sheds

Creamer's Dairy a vital part of Fairbanks history and landscape

The farmhouse and barns at Creamer's Dairy (constructed between 1905 and 1950 and now such an important part of the Fairbanks landscape) could easily have been lost. The dairy closed in 1966, the victim of changing market conditions and new health regulations that came about after statehood. At the same time, the city of Fairbanks was butting up against the formerly rural area and developers were eying the land for city expansion.

However, many people in Fairbanks rallied to save the farm from being subdivided. They saw the value in open space and enjoyed watching the annual waterfowl migrations. (The migrating birds were attracted to the grain found in the cow manure spread on the fields and also left in the fields after harvest.)

The booklet, *The History of Creamer's Dairy,* relates that local residents were able to convince state legislators and then Alaska Governor, Walter Hickel, to obtain state funding to purchase the land, but until funding was approved, the people of Fairbanks had to fend off eager developers.

Even in the wake of the devastating 1967 flood, the people of Fairbanks (through The Alaskan Conservation Society) were able to raise $7,000 as earnest money toward the purchase price of the farm. Charles and Don Creamer signed a purchase agreement in December of 1967 for 259 acres of the farm's land. The agreement did not include the 12 acres that the farmhouse, barns and other buildings sat on, since the amount the Creamers were asking was more than the buildings' appraised worth.

A combination of state and federal funds was finally approved in the spring of 1968 and used to purchase the land for the state of Alaska. In May of that year, the farm was put under the Alaska Department of Fish and Game's jurisdiction as the Fairbanks Wildlife Management Area. In 1970, an additional 1,520 acres of adjacent state land was added, bringing the total to about 1,800 acres.

The Creamers sold their remaining property to a land investment company in 1970. According to *A Place for the Birds*, a University of Alaska Fairbanks master's degree thesis, the new owners did little to maintain the buildings, using them primarily for storage. In fact, borough land records indicate that at one point they planned to tear down the farmhouse, which was in poor condition.

Fortunately for everybody, that did not happen. In 1977, the farm buildings were placed on the National Register of Historic Places (NRHP). The NRHP nomination form for the dairy emphasizes the buildings' importance, stating that it is "the only group of pioneer dairy farm buildings surviving in the interior of Alaska .

In 1979, the wildlife management area became part of the state refuge system and was renamed Creamer's Field Migratory Waterfowl Refuge. State funds were used to purchase the farm buildings and the 12 acres they sat on in 1982, adding the parcel to the refuge.

The farmhouse was renovated between 1988 and 1992, and the building is now used as an environmental education center. In 2001, the roofs of the barns and creamery were replaced, and a multi-year project was begun this year to renovate the barns and creamery.

Integral to the running of the education center and renovation of the buildings is the nonprofit group Friends of Creamer's Field. Established in 1990, the organization has worked with the Department of Fish and Game for more than 20 years to utilize the Creamer's Field refuge for environmental education and help preserve the farm's history. The organization is spearheading the current restoration project and hopes that, except for initial start-up funds from the state, all funding will come through private or corporate fund-raising.

Sources:

- *A Place for the Birds, The Legacy of Creamer's Field Migratory Waterfowl Refuge.* Jessica A. Ryan. Master's thesis, University of Alaska Fairbanks. 2003
- Conversation with William Holman, board president, Friends of Creamers Field
- Conversation with Mark Ross, education coordinator, Creamer's Field Migratory Waterfowl Refuge
- "Creamers Dairy National Register of Historic Places Inventory-Nomination Form." Alfred Mongin. National Park Service. 1975
- "Historic Structures Improvements Funding Request." Katie Watkins. Friends of Creamer's Field. 2012
- *The History of Creamer's Dairy. Robin Lewis.* Tanana-Yukon Historical Society. 1989

Desjardins-Stroecker Farm in 1995

Desjardins-Stroecker Farm representative of early Fairbanks agriculture

The Desjardins-Stroecker Farm, located at 2.5 mile on Farmers Loop Road, is one of the few remaining signs of the agricultural past in the Fairbanks area (besides Creamer's Dairy).

Gold may have been the impetus for bringing Westerners to the Chena River drainage in the early 1900s, but miners were not the only people attracted to the area. The history of agriculture in Fairbanks is almost as old as that of mining.

Homesteaders also arrived in Fairbanks on the early steamboats. According to a 1921 issue of *The Pathfinder*, one of the earliest was Klondike veteran Christian Heine, who established a homestead on Garden Island in 1903.

The book, *Historic Resources in the Fairbanks North Star Borough*, records that in 1908 there were 130 homesteads in the area, and by 1920 1,700 acres were being cultivated. The federal government was also quick to notice the agricultural potential of the area and in 1906 established an

Agricultural Experiment Station near where the University of Alaska would eventually be.

Early gardens and farms provided all the fresh produce for Fairbanks and the surrounding area. Before construction of the Alaska Railroad (ARR) all freight to Interior Alaska took months via steamer and riverboat. Even after the ARR completed a line to Fairbanks in 1923 the term "fresh" was relative.

The earliest farms and truck gardens were developed on the outskirts of the town: on Garden Island to the north, and to the south of 14th Avenue (present day Airport Way). As the city grew and land near town became more valuable, the farms and truck gardens moved to outlying areas such as Yankovich Road, Farmers Loop Road, Fairbanks Creek and Chena Hot Springs Road.

A bulletin published by the Alaska Agricultural Experiment Stations records that in 1911 Fairbanks area farms grew only 25 percent of the potatoes consumed locally, but by 1914 the local market was glutted, with 800 tons being produced. Grain crops were also successfully grown. The 1920 annual report for the experiment stations records that 6,000 bushels were reaped that year. The Interior proved so conducive to grain production that a flour mill was constructed in Fairbanks during the 1920s. Unfortunately, the mill burned down in the 1930s and was never rebuilt.

Farming became such an important part of the local economy and culture that the Tanana Valley Fair Association (now the Tanana Valley State Fair Association) was formed in 1924. Fairbanks first agricultural fair was held Sept. 11-13, 1924 on the playground at the city's public school.

Most of the early farms are gone, either absorbed by the city or subdivisions, or lying abandoned and overgrown. There are still some old farm buildings out in the hills, but the Desjardins-Stroecker Farm is perhaps the most visible.

Charles Desjardins, a French-Canadian, developed the farm. He was born at St. Arsene, Canada in 1870, and was one of the thousands who flocked to the Klondike in 1898. Desjardins mined in the Dawson City area until moving to Fairbanks in 1904, and mined in the Fairbanks area for several years before switching to farming.

In 1910 he began cultivating land along what was then called the "Farm Road." Desjardins filed for a homestead in 1914 and received patent to his land in 1924.

He was part of the area's bachelor farmer majority. This scarcity of women in farming was a recognized problem. The book, *Like a Tree to the Soil, a history of farming in Alaska's Tanana Valley,* relates that 50 bachelor farmers advertized in a San Francisco newspaper in 1919 for prospective wives--without appreciable results.

Desjardins raised potatoes, hay, produce and livestock until his death in 1926. Some of his fields were leased by Charles Creamer before World War II, and for many years the fields and buildings have been owned by the Stroecker family of Fairbanks, which is related to the Creamers.

Included at the site are three structures: a small log cabin, a barn which has a lower level of logs and an upper frame section, and the lower log courses of another structure which looks like it may have been a greenhouse. Although the farm buildings are no longer occupied the fields behind them are still cultivated.

Sources:

- *Historic Resources in the Fairbanks North Star Borough.* Janet Matheson & F. Bruce Haldeman. Fairbanks North Star Borough. 1981
- *Like a Tree to the Soil, a history of farming in Alaska's Tanana Valley, 1903-1940.* Josephine Papp & Josie Phillips. University of Alaska. 2007
- "Old Pioneer Laid to Rest," in *The Pathfinder.* November, 1921
- "Report of Work at Fairbanks Station," in *Report of the Alaska Agricultural Experiment Stations.* M. D. Snodgrass. USDA. 1920
- "The potato in Alaska," in *Alaska Agricultural Experiment Stations Bulletin 9.* H. W. Alberts. USDA. 1931

Eielson Memorial Building in 1997

Quirky Eielson building at UAF is an Art Deco gem

The University of Alaska, which was established in 1915 as the Alaska College of Agriculture and School of Mines, sits on a ridge with a commanding view of the Tanana and Chena River flats. The ridge's location made it a natural magnet for aboriginal peoples, who used the site for thousands of years to scout for game on the floodplain below. Several archeological sites are located on campus.

Adjacent to the Fairbanks Agricultural Experiment Station, the ridge was also a natural location for an agricultural college.

The first generation of campus buildings were all wood-frame, and no major structures survive from that time period. The second generation of campus buildings were reinforced-concrete structures. The Eielson Memorial

Building (with a modified Art Deco design) and the adjacent Signers' Hall (originally the university gymnasium) date from the mid-1930s.

The Eielson Building has a fascinating history to go along with its design. The building is named after Colonel Carl Ben Eielson, Fairbanks schoolteacher and pioneering aviator.

The book, *Polar Pilot; the Carl Ben Eielson story*, relates that in 1924 Eielson received the first air mail contract in Alaska, delivering mail from Fairbanks to McGrath. He is perhaps better known, though, for flying the first airplane across the Arctic Ocean in 1928. Later the same year he flew over Antarctica.

Eielson and his mechanic were killed in 1929 when their airplane crashed during a flight to rescue the passengers and crew of a three-masted schooner, the Nanuk, trapped by sea-ice off the coast of Siberia. (The Nanuk survived the winter and was later sold to MGM studios. It was used in Mutiny *on the Bounty, Treasure Island* and other movies.)

According to university records, sentiment in Alaska quickly turned to establishing a permanent memorial for Eielson. A committee representing the fraternal and civic organization in Fairbanks decided that a concrete building, the "Colonel Carl Ben Eielson Building of Aeronautical Engineering" should be constructed at the University.

The building, as originally designed, would have been an impressive structure: two stories plus daylight basement, 54-feet wide by 84-feet long, with Jacobian (17th Century English) embellishments and octagonal towers at the southwestern and northwestern corners.

Construction began in 1934 but the building committee quickly ran into problems raising funds and by 1935 only the first floor had been completed. The designers then modified their plans, simplifying the building.

When it was completed in 1940 it emerged as an Art Deco-style structure. It is still an impressive building (the same size as that called for in the original plans), and one of my favorites in the Fairbanks area. Incised rectilinear ornamentation flows around the cornice and exterior doors, and vertical grooving decorates the area below the windows on the first floor and at the tops of the pilasters.

The corner towers were never completed, but if you look closely the first floors of the towers are visible. The northwestern tower base is partially hidden by Siberian peas and other shrubs, but the southwestern base (sheltered by a large choke-cherry tree) is plainly visible from Salcha Street. The decorative metalwork on the fire-escape at the southern end of the building is also captivating.

Looking at the original architectural drawing, it appears the southwestern tower may have been planned as a stairwell. Now, the tower base is a large corner nook (housing the manager's small library) in the university's Office of Multicultural Affairs and Diversity.

All-in-all it's a quirky building with a quirky history, but I love it.

Sources:

- *American Architecture since 1789*. Marcus Whiffen. Massachusetts Institute of Technology. 1969
- Drawings and photos of Eielson Building, from Charles E. Bunnell Collection. University of Alaska Fairbanks, Archives
- "Carl "Ben" Eielson," in Farthest North Collegian. University of Alaska. June 30, 1930
- *The Cornerstone on College Hill*. Terrence Cole. University of Alaska Press. 1994
- "Carl Eielson Building," in UA Journeys online journal. Valerie Robancho-Andresen. University of Alaska Fairbanks. 9-28-2011
- "Nanuk' entry, in *H. W. McCurdy Marine History of the Pacific Northwest*. Gordon R. Newell. Superior Publishing Company. 1966
- *Polar Pilot: the Carl Ben Eielson story*. Dorothy G. Page. Interstate Publishers. 1992

Fairbanks - University of Alaska, Kuskokwim Way

Rainey-Skarland cabin in 2000

UAF's Rainey-Skarland cabin rich with history

Perched atop the ridge just north of the main section of the University of Alaska Fairbanks campus, the picturesque Rainey-Skarland Cabin seems slightly incongruous surrounded by modern buildings such as the Reichardt Natural Sciences Building, the Cutler Apartment Complex and the Moore-Bartlett-Skarland residence halls. However, the small cabin is still a cherished and important part of the university.

Froelich Rainey (the university's first professor of anthropology) and his wife had the cabin built in the summer of 1936. When they arrived at the university earlier that year, there was a shortage of housing. With the regents' permission, the couple's contractor erected a cabin in the woods about a half-mile above the campus.

University regents were understandably concerned about a private residence being built on campus. Consequently their approval came with the provision that the university had first purchase rights if the Raineys ever wanted to sell the cabin.

It was built in the American rustic style—a romantic vision of earlier pioneer dwellings that emphasized the use of natural materials and melding of structures into their surroundings. The three-room cabin (with basement) is carefully crafted from peeled logs and has unusual exterior design elements such as asymmetrical gable roof, pointed-arch living room window and plank doors with iron strap hardware.

The interior is just as distinctive, with its split-level design and massive stone fireplace in the center of the living room. Small clay figures tucked into the fireplace mortar, which are reminiscent of Dr. Rainey's earlier archaeological work in Haiti, also add to the cabin's eclectic charm.

The Raineys stayed in Fairbanks until 1942, and the university then purchased the cabin to use as faculty housing. A succession of faculty and visiting scholars, mostly in the department of anthropology, have since resided there.

According to the National Register of Historic Places nomination form for the cabin, residents have included a veritable who's who of northern researchers including Helge Larsen, J. Louis Giddings, Frederica de Laguna and Henry B. Collins. The most well-known (to Fairbanks residents at least) was anthropologist Ivar Skarland, who moved into the cabin in the late 1940s and lived there for 15 years.

A 2010 article published in the university's on-line journal, *UA Journey,* states that Skarland was a native of Norway and helped popularize Nordic skiing in Alaska. He was as well-known for his skiing prowess and hospitality as he was for his academic achievements, and his cabin, situated along the university's 30-mile long trail system, was a popular rest spot for people enjoying the campus trails.

He hosted numerous social events there, including annual Fourth of July parties, and "Ivar's cabin" became one of the social hubs on campus.

After he died in 1965, the university ski trail system and a residence hall were named in his honor. The Rainey-Skarland cabin was added to the National Register of Historic Places in 1975.

Skarland had several roommates during his tenure in the cabin, including Otto Geist, the pioneering northern paleontologist. I used to work with the curator of ethnology at the university museum in my student days, and she told me an amusing story (possibly apocryphal) about Otto.

Geist recovered bones and other remains of Pleistocene fauna from the Fairbanks Exploration Company's dredging operations and other mining activities. He apparently amassed a sizable collection of mammoth and mastodon tusks. I have seen photos of Otto's residence and its low fences built out of tusks and bones.

With nowhere to properly store the tusks, he supposedly sealed them in oil cloth and buried them somewhere on campus. No one had ever found them. It's possible that beneath the roots of some spruce tree near the cabin where Otto lived lies a small fortune in ivory tusks.

Sources:

- *American Architecture since 1789.* Marcus Whiffen. Massachusetts Institute of Technology. 1969
- "Cabin at core of UAF history." Tori Tragis. News release by University Relations, University of Alaska. March 2006
- "Historic Rainey Ridge Cabin to Get a Facelift," in *Fairbanks Daily News-Miner.* March 31, 1982
- *Historic Resources in the Fairbanks North Star Borough.* Janet Matheson & F. Bruce Haldeman. Fairbanks North Star Borough. 1981
- "History of the Rainey-Skarland Cabin." Valerie Robancho, in *UA Journeys,* University of Alaska. 2010
- Photo of tusk and bone fence from Otto Geist Collection. University of Alaska Fairbanks, Archives
- "Rainey's Cabin National Register of Historic Places Inventory-Nomination Form." Glenn Bacon. National Park Service. 1975

Appendix A
Identification key for animal tracks found at the bottom of some pages

Page 33	Ruffed grouse	
Page 37	Red fox	
Page 45	Snowshoe hare	
Page 51	Moose	
Page 53	Grizzly bear	
Page 65	Raven	
Page 67	Lynx	
Page 71	Wolverine	
Page 77	Gray wolf	
Page 81	Red squirrel	
Page 105	Gull	
Page 107	Caribou	
Page 115	Black bear	
Page 125	Vole	

www.ingramcontent.com/pod-product-compliance
Lightning Source LLC
Chambersburg PA
CBHW082041200426
43209CB00053B/1339